HOWZAT!

CHRISTOPHER LEE, former journalist and foreign correspondent, is one of Australia's leading television writers. He is the originating writer of many of Australia's most popular TV dramas including *Police Rescue*, *Big Sky*, *The Secret Life of Us* and *Rush*. He wrote the screenplays for the mini-series *Paper Giants: The Birth of Cleo* for the ABC and *Howzat! Kerry Packer's War* for the Nine Network. He has been awarded the Centenary Medal, four Australian Writers Guild Awards, the Queensland Premier's Literary ~~Award~~ ~~and~~ ~~the~~ ~~Fox~~ ~~Fellowship~~ for Screenwriting Excelle~~nce~~

HOWZAT!

KERRY PACKER
AND THE
GREAT CRICKET WAR

CHRISTOPHER LEE

Published in the United Kingdom by Old Street Publishing Ltd.,
Trebinshun House, Brecon LD3 7PX

Published in Australia by New South Publishing,
Sydney, NSW 2052

Design: Josephine Pajor-Markus
Cover Design: James Nunn

978-1-908699-45-9

Printed in the United Kingdom

10 9 8 7 6 5 4 3 2 1

First Edition

CONTENTS

PREFACE

Scriptwriters deal in small moments, building them into scenes, then sequences, then parts, and finally into some kind of coherent whole, a dramatic narrative. Directors and actors take over and... howzat! – a screen drama. With luck audiences are intrigued or reminiscent or frightened or repulsed – but, you hope, connected in some way to what's happening on screen.

Enter *Howzat! Kerry Packer's War*. At Southern Star Entertainment, after the 2011 success of *Paper Giants: The Birth Of Cleo*, a four-hour mini-series made for the ABC which introduced the character of Kerry Packer to TV drama, it was decided it'd be a good idea to do something more on this fascinating man. Research into Packer's war – the one he had with the cricket Establishment in the late 1970s, signing up the cream of the world's cricketers and setting up a whole anti-Establishment cricket system – showed that this guy and his cricket shenanigans were tailor-made for television. So a four-hour mini-series for the Nine Network went ahead.

But a *book* on Packer's war was an entirely different proposition. In the first place writing a book – although it mightn't look like it – is a different exercise than writing a screenplay. And secondly, and most importantly, apart from enjoying watching it, I know not much about cricket at all. The game is about weird things like popping creases and blockholes, third slips and silly mid-ons, flippers and chinamen, sweeps and hooks, the late swing and the early declaration.

But as it turns out, cricket is much more than what happens on the field. It involves all sorts of arcane rituals and Gordian thinking. With the exception of chess (which you could say is not a 'sport') the five-day game is arguably humankind's most complex and intricate sporting contest. Packer's 1970s war revealed a game and a time in its history that was gladiatorial, wonderful, filled with characters you couldn't possibly invent, moments of comedy, farce and true drama, all on top of a few centuries of rich anecdotal legend and myth.

Given all this, it struck me that a book on Kerry Packer's World Series Cricket need *not* be about the game itself. The elements of culture, conflict and character – a screenwriter's bread and butter – fill the story of Kerry and his iconoclastic band of sportsmen, so I thought I'd go with that.

I'd like to thank a series of people who helped out as I was putting first the screenplay then this book together, these absolutely indispensible players in the drama.

Firstly, John and Delvene Cornell, Ian and Barbara Chappell and Tony and Vivian Greig, who all helped out with generosity and charm. And I want to thank others who kindly shared their time and their reminiscences, notably David Hill, Bruce Francis, Allan Johnston, Bill Macartney, Trevor Kennedy, Geoff Longland and Richie Benaud. And researchers Stephen Vagg in Sydney and Hester Abrams in London.

I also want to sincerely thank that gentlemanly doyen of Australian cricket writing, Gideon Haigh and his encyclopaedic knowledge. His definitive book *The Cricket War: The Inside Story of Kerry Packer's World Series Cricket* is by any test the go-to volume for anyone wanting more detail on this fascinating chapter in cricket's history and I recommend it.

Finally, I'd like to thank my friend and colleague at Southern Star, the unsinkable John Edwards. We've been making television drama now for 26 years – and we're just warming up.

ABBREVIATIONS

ACB – Australian Cricket Board

CPH – Consolidated Press Holdings

ICC – International Cricket Conference

MCG – Melbourne Cricket Ground

NCC – New Zealand Cricket Council

BCCP – Board of Control for Cricket in Pakistan

SACA – South Australian Cricket Association

SCG – Sydney Cricket Ground

T20 – Twenty/Twenty cricket

TCCB – English Test and County Cricket Board

WACA – West Australian Cricket Association

WICBC – West Indies Cricket Board of Control

WSC – World Series Cricket

1
SET UP

At 2 pm on the sunny afternoon of Tuesday, 28 November 1978, thousands of people began queuing at the Sydney Cricket Ground gates to get into what would become one of the most significant cricket matches in the history of the game. Since Shakespeare's time the grand English sport had been played in the daytime, gradually developing over the centuries from a kid's game in English paddocks to an adult competition between locals, then villages, then shires, then as the British Empire covered the globe, internationally.

Ten months earlier, night cricket – cricket under lights – had been tried as an experiment in Melbourne by 'World Series Cricket', the organisation set up by businessman Kerry Packer to promote the sport on his TV stations. Night cricket in Melbourne had been enough of a success for a million dollars to be spent putting up six huge lighting towers round the Sydney Cricket Ground (SCG) – a million-dollar gamble that Melbourne had not been a fluke. If people came to this

1

SCG night game then cricket would never look back.

They did come. And how. So many people arrived that to save any kind of crowd mayhem, the gates were thrown open and a river of people flowed into the ground – women, men, kids, teenagers wanting to see their sporting heroes, young adults wanting to party, old farts wanting to see what all the fuss was about. They cheered and they sang and they laughed. As cricket crowds had done for centuries they applauded bowlers who took wickets, batsmen who scored runs and fielders who plucked impossible balls out of the air. They sang a new cricket anthem written especially for them, they ate and drank and enjoyed the night. Then they went home in the balmy evening and the huge lights went off.

This night had the cream of the world's cricketers out there on the field – Australians versus West Indians – champion sportsmen playing an intoxicating match. But the game had a greater consequence – it was a tipping point in the evolution of cricket. Behind lay many years of green and lovely English sporting drama. Ahead lay the day–night game, millionaire professional cricketers, the shifting of cricket's centre of gravity to the sub-continent and T20. After this sultry Sydney evening nothing about cricket would ever be quite the same again.

★

World Series Cricket (WSC) had its origins 18 months earlier when Kerry Packer, younger son of the fearsome Sir Frank Packer, Chairman of Consolidated Press Holdings (CPH), a media conglomerate and publisher of newspapers and magazines, decided he wanted to show cricket on his free-to-air network Channel 9. Kerry had taken the reins at the family company only two years earlier, in 1974, at the death of the old man. Long considered the 'idiot son' of Sir Frank, demeaned, belittled and bullied, often called 'boofhead' in public by his father, Kerry didn't waste any time as soon as Dad was safely in the grave. His big brother Clyde was the heir apparent, but unlike Kerry who always took the bullying silently, Clyde, the smart one, the chosen one, shoved back at his father and the two had quarrelled. Knowing the extent of the estrangement between Sir Frank and Clyde at the time of his father's death from cancer, young Kerry swept into CPH like a rat up a rope. According to Paul Barry, in his definitive 700-page biography of Kerry, the two brothers had a meeting and Kerry suggested coolly, 'I'd better buy your shares'. He did. Clyde handed over one-eighth of the family company to his little brother for $4 million and with one stroke was neatly cut out of what would soon become a conglomerate worth billions. Clyde took himself off to America where he started a publishing company, putting out mostly surfing magazines, gained massive amounts of weight and eventually died.

Chain-smoking, Fanta, Coke and milkshake-drinking, hamburger-loving Kerry didn't spend much time mourning his big brother; he was too busy building an empire. He hit the ground running, his first venture, begun just before his father's death, was the ground-breaking women's magazine *Cleo*. Under 35-year-old Kerry's stewardship and with magazine virtuoso, 30-year-old Ita Buttrose as editor, *Cleo* was a smash hit from the start, expertly surfing feminism's Second Wave. *Cleo* made money earlier, faster and more abundantly than anyone had thought possible. Kerry was on his way.

Kerry and Buttrose then revamped *The Australian Women's Weekly*, at one stage, *per capita*, the world's best-selling magazine. Begun in 1933 by his father, the old mag was now tired, dressed in yesterday's clothing – especially now that *Cleo* was on the scene – and losing readers fast. Kerry and Buttrose redid the format, cutting it down and giving it a more contemporary look. It was a huge gamble – a move that would character-ise Kerry's approach to business in years to come. *The Weekly's* readers were conservative, if not downright reactionary, skittish, averse to change and well used to the magazine's 40-year-old tone and style. Kerry's advice from various quarters was not to take the punt. Don't change horses midstream, if it's not broke, don't try to fix it, and so on. The chances were high that this would be Kerry's 'New Coke' – readers would take one sample of the new *Weekly* and keep their hands in their pockets.

But it paid off. Only months after Kerry and Buttrose's courageous move, *The Weekly* was selling a million copies a week and even more dollars were pouring into Kerry's shiny new coffers.

A man always interested in sport and by all accounts fascinated by and uncharacteristically humble in the presence of sportsmen, Kerry's next venture would be into the world of golf. He had boxed well at school, was a handy batsman and some-time wicketkeeper in Geelong Grammar's First XI and at his peak managed to get his golf handicap down to an impressive five. Later he would take up polo, his massive frame curiously in harmony with the tiny polo ponies he thrashed about the field. In 1975, hearing that the Australian Open Golf championship was on the lookout for a sponsor, Kerry slipped in with a quick $1 million offer to televise the Open on Channel 9 for three years. He then insisted that the Open be permanently housed at the Australian Golf Club in Sydney, in the same way the American Masters is always held at the Augusta National course in Georgia, and proceeded to tip another million into arranging for Jack Nicklaus – at the time the world's premier golfer – to re-design the course. The new layout didn't go down well with the world's professionals as they considered it ridiculously difficult. But Jack wasn't stupid, he loved it, and went on to win the first title easily. With Nicklaus as front man, innovative television coverage with cameras at every hole and more, Kerry's Australian Open was a smash both on the course and on television. He was on a definite roll.

And now it was cricket's turn. Kerry Packer decided to take his *Cleo,* his *Women's Weekly* and his golf experience into a wider and far more complex arena. Asked during the years he was involved in promoting cricket why he was taking such a close personal interest in the minutiae of the enterprise he said, 'My interest in cricket is no greater than if we were bringing out a new magazine … I'd be doing the same things for a new magazine, except that it would not be so visible or public'.

By simple fate he came into the game at a crucial moment in its history, three cricket planets were at the time moving into inexorable alignment and Kerry – one of the planets – found himself right there on the spot, ready to take advantage of the shift in the centre of the game's gravity. When these three planets were finally aligned there was nothing on earth that could stop a cricket revolution.

In early 1976, with colour TV being taken up at an amazing rate and cricket looking fresh and exciting on screen, Kerry decided to set out on his new journey and make his move into cricket broadcasting for Channel 9. He contacted the Australian Cricket Board (ACB) alerting them to the fact that he wanted to bid for the rights to Sheffield Shield and Test cricket. After the board had ignored him for four months – a ridiculous miscalculation on their part – he was finally called in to a meeting in June. Kerry smelt a rat as soon as he walked into the rooms of the Victorian Cricket Association (VCA) to meet with ACB Chairman 60-year-old Bob Parish and 59-year-old Treasurer Ray Steele.

Various accounts of the origins of World Series Cricket give different versions of this historic meeting. But however it happened, Kerry hit them quickly with a bid for $1.5 million for exclusive television rights. It was seven times what the Australian Broadcasting Commission (ABC) were paying and it took their breath away.

'After we recovered from the shock of his opening remarks and the amount of money, he was told there was no way we would consider exclusive rights because we had already entered into a commitment with the ABC,' Steele later told the British High Court.

According to Kerry, 'I had just walked in the door when Parish said they'd sold the non-commercial rights to the ABC. He knew why I was there – why I'd come to Melbourne. He knew too that I didn't want to share with the ABC. The ABC doesn't have to carry commercials and it's obvious even to Blind Freddie, that if you have a choice of watching the ABC without commercials or a commercial station, you watch the ABC. I told them I'd pay $1.5 million for a three-year exclusive contract when the ABC's contract expired in three years – I told them I'd sign there and then, half a million a year for three years. It was a lot more money than anyone had ever offered them – I knew that – I could tell by their looks'.

Kerry's tactic of blowing them out of the water with a blast of money should have worked. It's a tactic he learned well and used to perfection over the years.

But this meeting was more than a confrontation between three businessmen. Here in the elegant VCA room with its scattered historic cricket memorabilia and its sepia old cricketers glaring down from the walls, a classic encounter between generations was being played out – a confrontation between two old-school administrators and the restless, probing attitudes of a 1970s business tyro. Kerry was from a conservative moneyed background, brought up into privilege and always aware of his family's elite position, despite his father's rough edges and the old money claims that the family was still *nouveau*. Now, at last, he was doing it his way, understanding instinctively the changes that were sweeping Australia. The progressive Whitlam government had been comprehensively dumped only months earlier, but in four short years it had managed to usher in profound changes to the Australian political, social and cultural landscape that could never be undone. Kerry had nothing but contempt for Whitlam and his cronies, but he thought like them. He too was a man of the seventies. And Parish and Steele weren't.

After a little argy-bargy Kerry, losing patience, came to the point, taking one last shot with his famous quote: 'There's a little bit of the whore in all of us, gentlemen. Name your price'. Steele remembers the words as, 'We're all harlots. How much do you want?'

Kerry's version is better. It's more elegant with just the right touch of larrikin, missing in Steele's coldly direct wording. Whatever the words, Parish and Steele decided not to name their price. Possibly they later wished they had. Kerry stormed off and as the door closed behind him both men undoubtedly had the sinking feeling it wasn't a smart move to piss this young man off. As it turned out, planet number one had moved significantly into position. Kerry was willing to tear cricket apart to get his way.

The scene now changes to Neutral Bay, a middle-class suburb on Sydney's leafy lower North Shore, where 35-year-old John Cornell, a shrewd, baby-faced character born and bred in Kalgoorlie was living with his then girlfriend Delvene Delaney, a model and TV actress. (They later married – at midnight on New Year's Eve 1978 – 'easy to remember,' says Cornell.) He had moved as a young man to Perth from Kalgoorlie where he got a job as a journalist on the *Perth Daily News*, starting, coincidentally, on the same day as his friend Austin Robertson, known as 'Ocker', a Subiaco Football Club Australian Rules champion, and another young Perth wannabe named Michael Willessee.

Cornell and Willessee had quickly outgrown Perth and moved to Sydney to fulfil their individual destinies. They both fetched up at Channel 9 where Willessee became key man and star interviewer of *A Current Affair*, the channel's brand-new current affairs half hour, and Cornell was a producer. Also on *A Current Affair*, doing a short comedy skit at the end – and being paid just $50 for it – was an ex-Harbour Bridge rigger, Paul Hogan. Cornell, seeing Hogan and deciding he was 'the real deal' took over as his manager and the two men took off like rabbits. They established themselves as 'JP Productions' (J for John, P for Paul), and within a few years were making hundreds of thousands of dollars with *The Paul Hogan Show*, featuring Hogan as 'Hoges', a loveable larrikin in stubbies and workboots delivering blokey insights on Australia and its people beside his thick-as-a-brick best mate 'Strop', played by Cornell. And they brought in Delvene to play the dumb blonde. It's now part of Australian showbiz folklore how this clever trio created legendary television comedy out of playing three not-too-bright but you gotta love 'em, characters. Cornell, sharply intelligent, described playing the moronic Strop as 'part of my relaxation'.

By the time Austin 'Ocker' Robertson decided to abandon Perth and catch up with his friend in Sydney in 1976, Cornell, Hogan and Delaney were three of the hottest stars on the seventies telly. Robertson is often referred to as 'Austin Robertson Junior' because his father (at one stage a world champion professional sprinter) was also Austin Robertson. Robertson Junior was delayed in Perth because he was busy being an Australian Rules football hero. As a full forward for Subiaco he tallied up a West Australian National Football League record of 1211 goals, kicked more than 100 goals in a season six times and topped the goal-kicking record for a year eight times – averaging 4.8 goals per game. He mixed in elite sports company – by 1976 he was cricket superstar Dennis Lillee's manager and wanting to see if he could get the underpaid fast bowler a better deal from the game.

In 1970, D. K. (Keith) Lillee had been a young cricketer in a hurry. That year, at the age of 20, he began his first-class cricket career bowling for Western Australia, then quickly followed this up by taking 5–84 in his Test debut, the 1970–71 Ashes series. A year later, the young speedster announced to the world that something special had arrived – against a World XI that boasted Clive Lloyd, Garry Sobers and Sunil Gavaskar, he took 8 for 29. He then backed up in the Ashes tour of the following season in England by taking 31 wickets at the astounding average of 17.6. On the field this guy was terrifying the game's best batsmen, off the field he began forging superstar status as a broad-chested, broad-shouldered, floppy-haired sex symbol. With natural smarts, sheer pace and matinee idol looks, by 1976 Lillee was well on the way to establishing himself as a legend – and figuring he still had a way to go.

'Austin was staying with us at Neutral Bay and he asked me if I'd help manage Dennis Lillee,' said Cornell, 'So I said to Dennis "get a list of what you're charging at the moment, I mightn't be able to better it, but I might – and we'll see how we go". It was all very loose and friendly. Dennis put in a list and right at the top was "Nine months one week cricket – $8668". *Eight grand* for nine months of cricket when you're the best in the world? Well, this inflamed me. It's ridiculous – what are these people doing? I can get this for two nights entertainment from Hoges. It soon became clear the players were getting ripped off. For a Sheffield Shield match Dennis Lillee was paid slightly more than the guy moving the sightscreen. I was really pissed off about this so it became a bit of a crusade'.

John Cornell on a 'crusade' is a sight for the ages. The guy is a walking contradiction, boyish, blond, a thoughtful, self-contained larrikin with a steel-trap mind, a man of professorial judgment who, once he has decided on a course of action, will walk through walls. Christopher Forsyth, in his 1978 book on World Series Cricket, *The Great Cricket Hijack*, wrote, 'Though a calm, thoughtful character [Cornell] becomes a running knot of nervous energy when aroused. He enjoys the exchange of ideas and occasionally indulges in flippancy to hide the fact that he is an idealist with genuinely high standards, which very often lead him to doubting his own ability. He gets highly indignant when he sees or imagines people being cheated or hoodwinked and will make strenuous efforts to swing the balance their way. When told (later) that Dennis Lillee had been refused permission to park his car in his usual spot at the West Australian Cricket Association's ground in Perth, Cornell went white with anger. Fighting to articulate his feelings he burst out, "It … it just *lacks class*!".'

A few years later, Cornell and Hogan, completely under the radar, slipped over to the United States and did the celebrated 'Slip an extra shrimp on the barbie' TV ads for the Australian Tourism Commission. With Hogan's face a familiar sight all over America, in 1984 the two friends, along with TV comedy writer Ken Shadie, came up with the screenplay for *Crocodile Dundee*. Cornell and Hogan then backed themselves, turning *Croc Dundee* into a spectacular global success. As producer Cornell didn't pre-sell the movie to an overseas distributor – the normal practice. Sniffing that he had something special he held tight to his baby until it was finished. Only then did he do the deals. Thus he and Hoges (along with other partners including Kerry and a handful of World Series cricketers) effectively 'owned' the movie that went out and conquered the world. They cleaned up – *Crocodile Dundee* made a 730 per cent return to investors.

In 1976, Hogan and Cornell were still 'Hoges' and 'Strop', doing their TV gig, sitting round the Neutral Bay house plotting comedy for Channel 9 when they zeroed in on the idea of making some money for the players by slotting in extra cricket games at the end of each season. They figured why not add to the state-based Sheffield Shield and nation-based International Cricket setup. Get the ACB to arrange for the cream of the cricketers to simply play each other in a few matches – and the players would get most of the gate. The games would be based on the cricketers themselves and on the quality of cricket rather than on traditional state or district rivalries. Everybody on the field is a star. Everybody wins.

They zeroed in firstly on their star client Lillee, knowing just how badly the fast bowler was being treated by the game and its administrators.

'We had a meeting', says Cornell, 'and I said to Dennis, "Can we approach the board and ask for money to be paid to cricketers direct, have some games at the end of the year or something?" Dennis suggested some one-day games, but everyone said they couldn't trust the board – it was like a gentleman's club and it'd be a waste of time approaching them. So I said to Dennis, "We could put on some extra games for TV – how would you feel about that?" And he said, "I'll sign immediately and so would the rest of them".' Lillee then came up with a list of the Australian elite players who he assured them would jump at the chance to get involved.

Perfect. Cornell and Robertson went off to sound out the second necessary ingredient, 33-year-old Ian

Chappell, all-round tough guy and talented former Australian captain who had retired from international cricket the previous season but was still playing for North Melbourne. Chappell, who took over the Australian team in 1971 and retired after winning the Ashes in England in 1975, was the perfect man for his time, a resourceful batsman and master slips fieldsman who took no prisoners on the field or off. Chappell's aggressive larrikin charm took him into territory not many cricket captains ever dared to go. He sledged his opposition (he's sometimes credited with inventing sledging – the dishing out of insults and witticisms to batsmen at the crease), he took on the authorities for better conditions for his players, he said what was on his mind and he never took a backward step. Later WSC supremo Andrew Caro wrote 'his effort did more than any other to give World Series Cricket credibility'.

As Chappell tells it, 'I was living in Adelaide and flying to Melbourne to play club cricket. I'd basically just fly in what I was wearing, play cricket on the Saturday and then on the Sunday I'd fly back to Adelaide'. He was bored and immediately open to the suggestion that he captain Australia if the maverick idea ever got off the ground. But he also warned Cornell and Robertson not to try going to the ACB. With no chance of support from the official side of cricket, Cornell realised the program was going to have to be backed with a bit of healthy seed funding.

'That led me to thinking there's only one guy in Australia with balls big enough to tackle this and pockets deep enough – Kerry Packer. So I said to Dennis, "Do you know Kerry Packer?" And he said no, and I said, "have you ever heard of him?" And he said no. I said "Lillee, you are such a fucking provincial". He wasn't anywhere near as famous then as he is now.'

As producer of a highly successful Channel 9 comedy series, a show brought into the fold by Kerry himself, Cornell had a close enough professional relationship with Kerry to be able to kick his door in. Cornell walked into the office and asked Kerry whether he would like some top class cricket on Channel 9, complete with 'Dennis Lillee and the boys'.

'Well,' says Cornell, 'his eyes lit up.'

Kerry asked how the hell he was going to pull this off, so Cornell, warming to his theme, explained how he and Austin Robertson were managing Dennis Lillee, how Lillee had promised to sign up and how the rest of the best of Australian cricketers would almost certainly follow. 'Kerry responded with, "you'd better come back tomorrow, son".'

Why the 24-hour delay? Why didn't Kerry – eyes all alight – decide then and there to go for it? It was probably typical Packer not to leap in immediately. He knew instinctively that Cornell had brought him diamonds, yet he chose to send him away to mull for a while before making up his mind. It was a tactic, or at least a business strategy, learned from his father. One day was not going to make a bit of difference to this deal. But 24 hours of thinking might make a positive difference.

Kerry obviously slept well on the subject – as soon as Cornell walked into the office the following day Kerry's first words were, 'It's on'.

Kerry's view was that pissing round with just the Australian players wasn't milking the idea for all it was worth. Leading Australian cricket writer Gideon Haigh, in *The Cricket War*, the definitive book on World Series Cricket, describes Kerry's reply: 'Why not do the thing properly. Let's get the world's best cricketers to play Australia's best'.

Not just a game or two at the end of a season, or a 'test' match here and there, but a whole cricket tour played in parallel to the Establishment game. It was a stunningly audacious concept.

Cornell loved it, but immediately explained how he'd been warned the ACB would do its best to sabotage the deal if it got wind of what was going on and they'd be 'cut off at the pass'. The whole affair had to be kept under wraps while he and Robertson went about signing players.

'I said to Kerry, "can you keep secrets round here?" and he said, "we're the best in town at that, son".'

On that day the second planet moved into position. Kerry's pique against the ACB and the Cornell/Hogan/Robertson daring idea came into alignment. It just needed one more element – the cricketers themselves.

Cornell was amazed at the willingness of the players to sign up. And Kerry later told the English High Court it was 'frightening' the way the players swarmed to the idea. With Dennis Lillee making initial calls to the players who were then approached by Robertson, Cornell or both, the clandestine plan was quickly put into effect.

But why were the world's best cricketers so willing to turn their backs on the Establishment and risk their careers with the cricket boards? There was every chance in late 1976 that the whole thing would collapse, that the Establishment's livid – and expected – reaction would be spiteful enough to leave the top cricketers high and dry, their careers in ruins. They all signed with the knowledge that there was a good chance of being banned from first-class cricket forever. But seemingly without any second thoughts the young up-and-coming stars like David Hookes, happily signed alongside veterans like Ian Chappell and Rodney Marsh.

Why? Because the cricketers *were* getting ripped off. Royally. They had been for years, and there was a simmering resentment against the authorities who ran the sport. Throughout the 1960s and 1970s the players had watched elite golfers, footballers, hockey players, basketballers, baseballers – just about everyone else – finessing their sporting abilities into making millions or at the very least, serious money. By contrast, the world's best cricketers, not only in Australia but in England, the West Indies, India, Pakistan, New Zealand, were making something shy of the basic wage – for only part of the year. Rebellion was in the air. It was just a matter of time.

In 1978 Chris Forsyth described how Brian Taber, the Australian wicketkeeper for seven years, gave an example of the shabbiness of the rip-off. Taber reported that on the 1970 Australian tour of South Africa the ACB made a neat quarter of a million dollars profit (the money to be used for the benefit of Australian cricket), but when the team manager applied for a small $500 bonus for the players he was turned down flat.

There were many other examples. For the 1972 five-month, five-test Ashes tour the Australian players were paid a mere $2000 each. John Snow, a celebrated fast bowler who played for Sussex and England in the late sixties and early seventies spent the part of 1968–69 when he wasn't playing first-class cricket, on the dole.

A classic rip-off example involves the New South Wales and Victorian players in a four-day Sheffield Shield game in 1971. New South Wales won the match in three days, so none of the players got their $8 for the fourth day. There were stories of inedible food, miserly third-world accommodation, spouses banned from accompanying players on tour, tiny meal allowances. Everywhere they went Cornell and Robertson heard similar tales from disaffected players.

The cricketers' hostility to their boards, growing for years, reached a new height just a year earlier in 1975 when the successful and immensely popular Australian Test players felt they deserved an increase in match payments. The reply from the ACB Secretary Alan Barnes brought the players to white-hot anger. 'These are not professionals,' he said, 'They were invited to play, and if they don't like the conditions there are five hundred thousand other cricketers in Australia who would love to take their places.'

It was the same all over. The cricket boards of the world were treating their chief income-earners like lab rats.

Now the planets were fully aligned. The third element – the players' disaffection – brought about critical mass. The moment Cornell and Robertson fronted the players with written contracts their eyes lit up like Kerry's and they reached for a pen.

First to join up was, of course, Dennis Lillee. In January 1977, during a Sheffield Shield game between Western Australia and South Australia, he signed a three-year contract worth a total of $105,000. Obviously it made him a very happy boy – that same day he ripped into the South Australian batsmen taking 5 for 44. Cornell and Robertson then went off cherry-picking the finest cricketers around the globe. World Series Cricket was born. For the next three years the game was in for a bumpy ride.

★

Because he was slated to be captain and a major selector along with Kerry, Ian Chappell was called to the inner sanctum. 'I remember flying in to Melbourne one day and there was a message waiting for me', he says, 'It was from Austin Robertson. "Jump on the next plane to Sydney. You've got a meeting with Kerry Packer".'

'So I jumped on this plane and flew to Sydney. I had a pair of jeans on and a cowboy shirt and a denim jacket. I went in and Kerry had this bloody sort of chair that used to tilt way back and he had his feet up on the desk with no shoes on. When I walked through the door there was no hello how are you or anything like that. He just said,"What are you? Some sort of fucking cowboy, are you?"'

'Then it was, "Okay, who do you want on this fucking team?" I said, "Hang on Kerry, I'm not the captain. My brother Greg's captain of Australia".'

'"What do you think this is, a fucking democracy?" he says, "I'm paying the bills – I'll pick the captain. You're the fucking captain. Now who do you want on the fucking team?"'

'I said, "Well look – just so we don't have a family problem here, can I at least make a phone call before you start announcing I'm the captain?" So I rang Greg and said, "Kerry wants me to captain the side". He said, "Mate, I've had it for two years – it's a bastard of a job. You're welcome to it".'

Kerry had made the right choice for the culture he had in mind for World Series Cricket – fast, attractive, tough, take-no-prisoners. Playing against a team with Ian Chappell as captain has been described as turning a cricket match into gang warfare.

With a player of Chappell's stature on board and with Dennis Lillee riding shotgun, Cornell and Robertson set about spending Kerry's money. Between Lillee's signing on 10 January and the Australia/England Centenary Test in early March 1977, they managed to sign nine of the top Australian cricketers – the laconic champion batsman and part-time bowler Doug Walters, a man deeply loved by the Australian cricket public, plus Ian Redpath, Ross Edwards, Max Walker, Rick McCosker, Kerry O'Keefe and Greg Chappell.

Cornell and Robertson were chary of the younger Chappell. Unlike his rough-and-ready older brother, Greg Chappell was neat, clean, careful. He has been described as well organised, even schoolmasterish, known for his probity and integrity. They knew that if anyone was going to go off and warn the Board it would be this guy. It would be a gamble, but after pondering for some time they finally decided to risk it and take a punt on him. Show their hand and hope for the best.

'So I went to his hotel room one night and sat down and talked for 20 minutes straight laying all my cards on the table, with him looking at me without the expression on his face changing one bit', says Cornell, 'You couldn't tell whether he was going to be in it or not. You couldn't tell whether he was going to run off to the board immediately as Australian captain and report it all.'

'In the end I looked at him, he looked at me, and he said, "Count me in".'

They sighed with relief and plunged on, buoyed by the fact that in their cat-and-mouse game with the ACB not one word was leaking out.

★

The immortal Centenary Test arrived, beginning on 12 March 1977, and the ACB organised the contest as one befitting its historic importance. More than a hundred past players and 'legends' from all over the world were invited to Melbourne to be wined, dined and showcased in a cricket jubilee that went for nearly two weeks. This was cricket at its zenith, described by one newspaper headline as 'Cricket's Finest Hour'. As the old men gathered to reminisce, the game was never stronger, the anecdotes never funnier, the days of heroism and pain never more sharply recalled. Cricket was more than a game, it held all the idiosyncratic twists and turns, all the pain and the triumphs, of life itself.

And just to prove them right, the Centenary Test turned out to be a game for the ages, filled with many of the elements that make cricket such a unique sporting contest. Aficionados of the game will tell you this historic drama, played at the Melbourne Cricket Ground (MCG) – the same venue as the first Test in 1877 – was one of the most enduringly fascinating cricket matches ever held. On day one the huge crowd saw Australian batsman Rick McCosker slump to the ground when a bouncer from Bob Willis dropped him like a left hook.

He had been slowly building an innings when a fast-rising ball caught him unexpectedly, smashing his jaw. On day three, to help consolidate Australia's lead, he returned to the crease, walking out onto the field in sunshine with his jaw wired up and his head swathed in white bandages. The crowd sang 'Waltzing McCosker'.

Young batsman David Hookes, blond and boyish, was only 21, untried at Test level but with many of the Australian team predicting great things from him. He set himself, got his eye in, then announced his arrival at international level by belting England captain Tony Greig for five consecutive boundaries. The very next ball he was bowled by Derek Underwood.

In the first innings Dennis Lillee took an incredible 6 for 26. Then, in pain from a troublesome back and bowling on a completely dead wicket, he fronted up in the second innings and took 5 for 139.

During England's second innings, England number three Derek Randall had one of those days batsmen will tell you happen on rare occasions. They see the ball coming out of the bowler's hand and know exactly where it will land, their feet move magically into place, the ball arrives large as a melon, their bat is a foot wide…

Randall, a bouncy, high-octane player and personality, who'd never really done much in international cricket, swept through his first-ever Test century then plunged happily on through his 150, making it look for all the world as if he was going to take England to the win. With his score at 161 he was caught behind by Rodney Marsh. The crowd went crazy – this was the death-knell for England. But Marsh shook his head and indicated to the umpire he hadn't taken the catch cleanly. The game was back on a knife-edge.

Randall finally went for 174. As he traipsed off to a standing ovation, grinning and waving at the crowd, the game was all but over. Lillee continued bowling, taking wickets, and his final, unplayable straight fast ball trapped Alan Knott LBW. Australia won by 45 runs – the exact same margin they had won in 1877.

The match went down in history only partly because of the action on the field. At the moment of the game's greatest triumph cricket had a worm in its entrails. The Australian dressing room after the game was a scene of triumphant jubilation, the players drinking long-necks of beer, laughing, congratulating each other – and mixing happily in there with them were Bob Parish, Ray Steele and a handful of other cricket administrators. Like some character out of a cheap spy movie Austin Robertson walked in carrying a briefcase. It held $75,000 in cheques. As Parish and Steele looked on, vaguely wondering what this was all about, Robertson moved amongst the players handing them their initial

WSC payments. 'Here's your theatre tickets, guys!'

'That's how we did it', he said later, 'and though it seems unbelievable, no one suspected a thing.'

Kerry now needed to lock up his overseas players, starting with the most important of them all, Tony Greig, riding high in popularity in England and Australia after coming so close to winning the Centenary Test. Austin Robertson teed up the meeting and Greig flew to Sydney.

On 22 March 1977 Tony Greig walked into Kerry's office with his friend and business manager 29-year-old Bruce Francis, a handy, popular batsman who had batted for New South Wales and Essex and had even played three test matches for Australia. As it happened these three had a conversation at a social function a year earlier about cricket on TV. Kerry had been, even then, mulling over how best to maximise sport on his network.

As Greig tells it, as soon as he entered the office Kerry offered him $30,000 a season for three seasons. To any other cricketer this was gold. But Greig was unique amongst the players, way ahead of his time, already making good money from his 'brand' and soon to be the world's first cricket millionaire. Thanks partly to Francis and partly to his own entrepreneurial abilities, he was spruiking Kellogs, Waltons, *The Australian Women's Weekly*, Golden Books and the airline TAA. He was well paid on the speakers' circuit and well connected all over. Mick Jagger had already agreed to appear at a Tony Greig benefit concert at Wembley Stadium – a gig that, if it came off, had the chance of making Greig a fortune.

With this as leverage, Greig prised from Kerry an extra $10,000 for being the WSC World captain. He then negotiated 'a job for life' working for CPH and a low-interest housing loan in case he left England and decided to buy a place in Australia. The previous season he had played for Waverley in Sydney, living in Vaucluse and loving the Australian lifestyle. Kerry acceded to all this then asked if he wanted any more 'licks of the lolly'. Francis did. He wanted Kerry to give a personal guarantee, in writing, that Greig would get every penny.

That was it. The famous Kerry temper came bubbling up.

'Where did you fucking find him?!' he said, pointing at Francis, 'There wouldn't be a businessman in Sydney – or Australia for that matter – who wouldn't accept my personal guarantee. I sold the Telegraph to Murdoch for sixteen million in the back of a car, and here I've got a snotty-nosed kid wanting my guarantee in writing for a lousy forty grand a year. You and your mate have got to be fucking kidding.'

Francis kept pushing and Kerry's displeasure rose. He whirled on Greig.

'Is your fucking mate deaf or just fucking dumb?' he asked, 'If you two want to play big businessmen you can go into that room next door and pore through the contract. I promise you it's not bugged. You can keep me waiting an hour or two and pretend I'm in here trembling about whether you're going to sign or not. Then when you've finished your silly games you can come back and sign the fucking thing'.

It took Greig a week of agonised soul-searching, but in the end he signed – also agreeing to act as recruiting officer in collecting the World team. It was a courageous decision. This guy had a lot to lose, more than any of the others. He knew he was taking his career and his hard-earned good name into unknown, dangerous territory.

A short time later, Greig and Robertson signed up the charismatic and Hollywood-good-looking Pakistani paceman Imran Khan and his cousin Majid, plus Pakistan vice-captain and veteran batsman Asif Iqbal and the popular Mushtaq 'Mushie' Mohammad.

Then came another jewel in the crown. Only 33 but already venerable, Clive Hubert Lloyd, known as 'Hubie' or 'Supercat' to the cricketers, also signed for $90,000 for three years. Tall, bespectacled, hunched and awkward, Lloyd doesn't look anything like an elite sportsman. He slouches to the crease wearing glasses and carrying a bat most people would have trouble lifting (he built himself up by pressing weights as a kid), then proceeds to pound bowlers to all parts of the ground. No matter how fast the ball, Hubie always seemed to have all the time in the world to decide what to do with it. The cricketers will tell you when Lloyd was having a good day there was simply nothing to be done but run about like chooks trying to cut off fours. Lloyd began his first-class cricket career for Guyana in 1963 and had been captain of the West Indies since 1974. In 1976, he equalled the then record for the fastest double-century in first-class cricket by belting 201 not out in 120 minutes for the West Indies against Glamorgan. Without raising a sweat.

Lloyd was brought up in struggletown. His father – who died when Lloyd was 14 – a chauffeur to a local doctor. Young Clive was bright, worked hard at school, went to the Anglican Church every Sunday, and lived for cricket. Without money for the entrance fee to local cricket fields Clive and his mates would watch the games on a 'bird ticket' – from the branches of trees outside the ground. (Australian cricketers used to enjoy trying to hit a six into the trees. The kids would see the ball coming and drop to the ground in bunches.)

When he started playing cricket in Guyana there was unofficial segregation in the country – white and Portuguese played for one club, blacks for another – and young Clive took note.

Unlike most of the other West Indian players, Lloyd, grave and soft-spoken, was able to articulate his black conscience. He was inspired by Hollywood actor Sidney Poitier who broke new ground for black actors in the sixties, and the heroic West Indies cricketers of the generation before him. 'I loved the way Poitier strutted when he walked, in the same way I loved the way Garry Sobers walked to the wicket, the way Wes Hall marked out his run up. These things influenced me because these men were saying, "We're on our way up". Seeing those things was as important to me, as influential and memorable, as seeing our flag go up for the first time or seeing a black prime minister in the Caribbean. They showed that we were moving somewhere. My ancestors, Garry Sobers' ancestors, Wes Hall's ancestors, they all came from Africa. My real hope is that the countries where these people were taken from will one day become great cricketing countries.'

As he grew in stature in the game, Lloyd saw clearly the politico-cultural side of being captain of West Indies cricket. 'When I made a decision of consequence as the West Indies captain,' he once said, 'it was of more importance than any one prime minister in the Caribbean. They were only making decisions for one territory – I was making them for the whole of the West Indies'.

He went further, understanding the racially historical

dimension of cricket in the West Indies, a game handed down to the black people of the string of islands by its colonial masters, the English. The people of the Caribbean saw themselves as discrete groups, but Lloyd railed against inter-island rivalry and from 1974 to April 1977, when he signed with WSC, he forged his West Indies players into a complete whole, developing team harmony by mixing the guys up, rooming players from different islands in with each other, putting junior players with senior ones, batsmen with bowlers. He kept control by being the 'the leader', the father figure, consciously forging a team of terrifying effectiveness and pride. His players, legends such as Viv Richards, Joel Garner, Andy Roberts, Gordon Greenidge, Michael Holding and Roy Fredericks (all of whom signed with WSC) were gifted, natural sportsmen, but still Lloyd, particularly after the genesis of WSC, insisted on a punishing regimen of physical fitness and cricket training. And to his notorious late-night party men he introduced a curfew. Be on the bus in the morning or else. Lloyd's team bus never waited more than five minutes after its scheduled departure time. When the bus pulled away from the hotel, heading to yet another great cricket ground, it held the most fearsome and glorious cricket team the world had ever seen.

With a man of Lloyd's pre-eminence on board it

was a simple matter for Greig and Robertson to sign up the other West Indians on their list – all they had to do was tell them Hubie had joined up and the players would grab for the pen. There was just one hiccup. Fast bowler Michael Holding – the man credited with the most flowingly beautiful run up and delivery on any cricket field ever – heard that WSC would include South Africans. Holding was Jamaican and acutely aware his government had banned all sporting links with Apartheid South Africa. He insisted, and got, a special escape clause that could nullify his contract – just in case.

In the early seventies, the official South African team, made up entirely of white-skinned players, was only authorised to play what were considered *white* nations – England, Australia and New Zealand. Top South African cricketers Eddie Barlow, Mike Procter and Barry Richards had immediately taken off for England where they all flourished in English County cricket. Greig, who had been playing against them in Britain, wanted all three, as well as champion batsman Graeme Pollock and legspinner Denys Hobson.

At this point, the top-secret WSC had its first dodgy moment. When Hobson, Richards, Barlow, Procter and Pollock all (paid for by Kerry) got on a London-bound plane to talk to Greig, nosey South African journalists started sniffing around. Five champion cricketers all heading off together? Why? What's going on? And things got dodgier still when the South African Sunday Times reported that four of the cricketers had 'signed lucrative contracts to play an eight-week series of matches throughout the world'. But the story quickly faded, the journalists were easily convinced that the players had vague County Cricket obligations in Britain. And besides, the story stayed in South Africa – none of the international wire services could confirm it. In London in April 1977 all five signed on.

Champion Australians such as wicketkeeper Rodney Marsh, lightning-fast bowler Jeff Thomson, and the young tyro David Hookes also signed on, as did top English players like veteran fast bowler John Snow and wicketkeeper Alan Knott. By the end of April 1977, WSC had 18 Australians and 17 international players. Thirty- five. The cream of the world's cricketers. All done behind a wall of silence – not a word had leaked out.

In another strategic move, Kerry, obviously thinking in the longer term, signed up two of cricket's elder statesmen Richie Benaud and Sir Garfield Sobers.

At the time he was recruited, Sir Garfield St Aubrun Sobers was only 41 but already a knight. He was a freakish all-round player who could bat sublimely, bowl spin and fast-medium and an astonishing fieldsman who could with no apparent effort flick a ball 70 metres to an inch over the bails. Benaud has described him as 'the greatest all-round cricketer the world has seen'. A popular man with a gap-toothed grin, a dual citizen of Australia and Barbados, 'Garry' made his first-class cricket debut at the age of 16, then went on to successfully captain the West Indies. In 1968 he became the first batsman in history to hit six sixes from one over, a sensational feat once considered impossible at the top level but one cricketers had secretly aspired to for the past 100 years (it's been done three times since, but only once more in first-class cricket, the others were in a one-dayer and a twenty-over T20 match).

Richie Benaud was only 22 when he made his Australian Test debut back in 1951–52 against the West Indies, starting slowly and unspectacularly then flowering into one of the great forces of Australian and world cricket. Like Sobers he was a batsman, a spin bowler and an outstanding fieldsman, but it was his aggressive, tactical captaincy that made him legend. And his character. Benaud's forceful personality meant that his troops would follow him straight into the jaws of hell, and the cricket public straight through the turnstiles. He made a successful career as a cricketer, retired as Australian captain in 1964 then went on to become one of the game's iconic radio and TV commentators. Gideon Haigh has described him as 'perhaps the most influential cricket personality since the Second World War'.

Alongside his wife Daphne, Benaud ran a sports consultancy business. In early April 1977 he met Kerry in his office and was asked if his company would represent WSC. Benaud said later he had difficulty believing that the whole thing had been kept under wraps for so long. Richie and Daphne plunged in, quickly becoming a highly efficient and indispensible part of the WSC administrative machine. Richie, master diplomat and cool guy, danced elegantly along the fine line between the rebel WSC and the Establishment, the man who knew the opposition from the inside, who could think like them, who could give invaluable advice on tactics and strategy. WSC heavies still eulogise Benaud's part in the success of the whole enterprise, though Benaud himself modestly brushes off the praise.

Sobers, meanwhile acted as elder statesman and *eminence grise*, bringing the formidable power of his name and presence to the organisation. At press conferences, journalists would not be fronting up just to speak with Kerry, the man seen as the destroyer of cricket. They would be faced with Kerry, John Cornell, Tony Greig, plus the gravitas of Sobers and Benaud. World Series Cricket packed an awful lot of firepower up front. When the story finally broke, the Establishment knew immediately it was not dealing with some greedy Aussie businessman and bunch of rat-arsed sportsmen. One look at Benaud and Sobers and the world's cricket authorities knew they had a major schism on their hands.

★

As with many aspects of WSC, the exact details of how the story finally broke is shrouded in mystery. Who was the person who blabbed to the press? All reports agree that whoever it was, he had been doing quite a bit of drinking at a barbecue on the evening of Saturday, 7 May, put on by Tony Greig and his wife Donna at their grand UK Brighton home for the Australian players in England for the mid 1977 Ashes series. The party started off with a bang, more than a hundred people of the cricket world assembled at the home of the popular England captain under marquee lights in his large back-yard, drinking champagne and Fosters beer through the damp night, cricket enemies enfolded by camaraderie and a love of the game. But at some critical moment the mood changed. Word spread like a virus that a couple of reporters had blown the story wide open – the World Series genie was out of the bottle. The party turned into something like the military high command's whispering inner sanctum on the eve of major war.

It's best told by Henry Blofeld, at the time the doyen of British cricket writers, in his book on WSC, *The Packer Affair*.

'It was at that party,' he writes, 'that Greig and the other Packer players heard that their plans were about to be published in Australia. There were about 150 people in the marquee in Greig's garden and the party was in full swing, according to one of the guests Alan Lee of the *Sunday Telegraph*, Greig even had a bottle of champagne in his hand when he was told. He was naturally greatly concerned, and the party rapidly developed into a council of war as those involved gathered in whispering groups. Those who did not know what was happening could not understand what was going on, and the night was full of furtive, sidelong glances; by the end it was apparently difficult to distinguish those who knew from those who did not.'

The two journalists credited by history with breaking the story – one of the great scoops of sports reporting – were Australians Peter McFarline writing for the Fairfax papers *The Age* and the *Sydney Morning Herald*, and Alan Shiell a former Sheffield Shield batsman for South Australia, reporting for News Limited's the *Daily Telegraph* and *The Australian*. The pair had been sniffing round the story for months and getting nowhere. Any mention of a rebel cricket tour brought immediate denials from anyone they spoke to. But like the experienced newsmen they were, they kept digging, sniffing, pooling their intelligence, knowing they were onto some kind of great revelation. They'd got their latest denial just that morning from Greg Chappell. When McFarline and Shiell buttonholed him in a corridor outside the Australian dressing room Chappell had listened politely then replied with, 'You can say this: "It sounds an interesting proposition – I'd like to know more about it".' McFarline said that at the time Chappell had 'only a hint of a smile on his face'.

The two reporters arrived at Tony Greig's house that night, notebooks in hand, knowing that alcohol was their secret weapon. Beneath the coloured lights they chatted amiably with various Australian players, probing, probing. Blofeld later reported that Alan Shiell had got the story from an Australian player and 'although Shiell was evasive about which one, it was thought to have been David Hookes, who was known to have had serious doubts about the wisdom of signing for Packer'.

When they decided to secretly file their articles to Australia on the night of the Brighton party, bringing the whole wall of silence crashing down, McFarline and Shiell were writing vague detail and speculation put together from snippets of half-information. Later they were gobsmacked at how big the story really was.

McFarline wrote that he and Shiell had 'pieced together the broad outline' of WSC but that 'neither of us quite realised its extent, even by the time we came to break the story from Hove on 7 May 1977, in time for the morning papers in Australia on 9 May'.

The morning of Monday, 9 May 1977 was sunnier in Sydney than it was in Brighton. Knowing the shit was about to hit the fan, Tony Greig rang Kerry with the news, then decided to issue a press statement which prompted more questions than it answered. 'There is a massive cricket project involving most of the world's top players due to commence in Australia this (northern) winter,' it said, 'I am part of it, along with a number of English players. Full details and implications of the scheme will be officially announced in Australia later this week.'

The Fleet Street reporters, comprehensively scooped, had to let fly with what they had. The news was so hot it swept off the sports pages onto the front pages of the world's newspapers and dominated radio and television news bulletins. The *Daily Mail's* Ian Wooldridge who, like McFarline and Shiell, had been digging away for months and had been fast closing on the full story, was the best-informed of the English journalists. Under the banner headline *'World's Top Cricketers Turn Pirate'*, Wooldridge described the 35 rebel players as 'dogs of cricket' but went on to say '... far from being a shock development, I suggest that the only surprise about what happened at the weekend was that it was so long delayed. If the game's administrators failed to see it coming, then they are low in perception'.

Wooldridge's editorial attitude was one point of view, the one shared by the cricketers who had signed up, and also by Kerry and Cornell. A short time later a similar stance was taken by President of the West Indies Cricket Board of Control (WICBC), Jeff Stollmeyer: 'I don't see how anyone can condemn the players. After all, their careers are not all that permanent. I do not think that in the longer term that exhibition matches will attract either the interest or the gates that Test matches will'.

But voices like these were drowned out by the shrill response from most of the rest of the press. And besides, Stollmeyer didn't quite get it. The WSC administrators and especially the rebel players always railed against use of the term 'exhibition matches' to describe the World Series program of Supertests and One Day games. These games were *not* dinky 'exhibitions'. The players saw the whole WSC sporting venture as stimulating, significant cricket, justifiably as appealing to the public as any of the Establishment games. The cricketers will tell you it's the hardest cricket they ever played. They were out there naked in the blazing sun, facing bouncers, standing at

'silly' fielding positions, throwing themselves dangerously at flying balls, crashing into pickets trying to cut
off fours just as cricketers had always done. Any suggestion that they were phoning it in made their blood boil.
In his autobiography Viv Richards describes the WSC
game as 'gladiatorial cricket at its finest'. 'Forget the
press stories,' he wrote, 'it was far from shoddy. It was
top-class, dangerous, intense, beautiful cricket'. Stubborn bastards at best, the players dismissed the 'exhibition' suggestion by consciously turning WSC into a fast,
mad and cut-throat game. And, ultimately, this was just
what the punters wanted to see.

In his judgment later that year in the English High Court
on the dispute between WSC and the Establishment, Mr
Justice (Sir Christopher) Slade said, 'The news became
public on 9 May 1977 and caused great consternation
amongst the governing bodies for cricket...'

Sir Christopher was a man given to understatement.
The 'great consternation' took the form of hysterical
editorials in newspapers, snarling from cricket authorities all over the globe and dire warnings by commentators and old boys that the noble game was being holed

beneath the waterline. Cricket was 'at a crossroads', cricket was facing the greatest peril in its hundred-year history, cricket had met its 'Pearl Harbour', the entire game was 'under threat' by 'pirates', etc, etc. In London, senior commentator John Arlott came up with the term 'circus'. But BBC commentator Christopher Martin-Jenkins pulled out the best metaphor: 'For those of us who admittedly take the game too seriously,' he wrote, 'it was like learning that a wife whom one loved and trusted had been secretly, and for some time, making love to another man'.

All of which was true to a lesser or greater degree. Cricket had been quietly admiring itself in its ivory tower, but now the barbarians had arrived at the gates.

Nothing before or since has hit cricket – or any sport – with such an explosive impact. David Hill, the genius behind the close sound and the multi-camera coverage of the game, who later exported his innovative expertise to sports in the United States and beyond, described the arrival of WSC as 'the most astounding chapter in the entire history of world sports'.

By contrast a little graft and corruption here and there, bribery and match-fixing, stained the game in the twenty-first century, but no one ever suggested the global organisation was critically wounded by such activity or had come to any kind of crossroads. The nefarious dealings of a handful of Pakistani cricketers, caught taking bribes to under-perform or to bowl no balls at specific moments in Test matches, had no impact on the gates and brought about very little Armageddon comment in the press. A few players jailed and barred from the game... see you later guys, now let's get on with it.

Much of the frothing reaction from the Establishment cricket press was over the secrecy that Kerry and his clan of players and administrators had managed. How dare this man sign all these players up and not tell anyone! Lucky it all leaked out or no one would know! When was he going to announce it – on the very eve of next year's Test matches?

The truth is Kerry had already come clean and written to the ACB, giving them the outline of the whole thing. In one of those fine ironies of history, Richie Benaud had drafted a letter to Bob Parish in April, which was couriered on 5 May, the previous Thursday, and supposed to be hand-delivered on the Saturday, 7 May – the night of Tony Greig's Brighton party. But an air strike had held it up and Parish read the story in the paper the following Monday before the letter got to him that evening. With the cat out of the bag, Kerry did his best to at least ameliorate the situation.

'I rang him and apologised because the letter had not reached him before the story became public,' Chris

Forsyth quotes Kerry as saying. 'I asked to come to Melbourne to talk about it and then work out a compromise. But he virtually told me there was no purpose in that.'

Kerry was wrong-footed, so – never more Kerry – he went on the attack. He held a series of truculent television interviews for the night's news, telling a journalist who queried the effect WSC might have on the game, 'Cricket is going to get revolutionised whether they like it or not. There is nothing they can do to stop me. Not a goddamn thing.' And with consiglieri John Cornell sitting beside him, giving nothing away, he faced the Sydney print press, coming up with one of the most oft-quoted lines in the whole saga. 'We'll do all we can to co-operate with the Cricket Board and, if they co-operate with us there's no reason why Test cricket, as it is now, will be affected,' he said, 'But if they don't co-operate they'll walk straight into a meat mangler.'

In contemporary reports it's sometimes a meat 'grinder' – but you get the idea. Kerry then went on to give the cost of the whole venture up to that point as $2.5 million. He talked about the severity of the players' professional contracts and what he expected of his 35 players and said he'd be seeking to play on the Establishment cricket grounds, but if they weren't forthcoming they'd be playing happily elsewhere.

And in another example of fine aggression, his reaction to the enemy's dismissive insults was to open another front. Kerry, Cornell, Greig and the other insiders decided they were in so much hot water they might as well go for broke. Why not keep signing – that'll get up the noses of the Establishment – and have a three-cornered contest. Not just Australia versus The World, but with a full West Indies team tossed in there as well? Kerry okayed the spending of another huge lump of money and the guys went off on a second recruitment drive. They plundered the West Indian team and into the fold came the classiest of the West Indians – Roy Fredericks, Lawrence Rowe, Gordon Greenidge, Albert Padmore, Deryck Murray, Collis King, Wayne Daniel, Bernard Julian, Alvin Kallicharran and the giant fast bowler Joel Garner. By the middle of June that year Kerry had 49 of the world's best players – three full teams, with change.

Meanwhile the cricket authorities, especially in England, having got over their initial shock of the announcement, went out hunting, looking for someone to blame. And right in their cross-hairs they found Tony Greig, the perfect fall guy – suddenly it was open season. Born in South Africa but now an Englishman, Greig had taken over the captaincy of a struggling and haphazard English team in 1975, led them to a decisive Test series victory in India, then narrowly lost the Centenary Test in Melbourne. He had achieved this more by way of courage, determination and strength of character than any God-given gift of cricket brilliance. A batsman, bowler, top fielder and canny leader, he was blond, six foot six inches tall and at the very peak of his game and his popularity, well known and even loved by the cricket public in Britain, India and Australia. This despite a few blots such as an incident in Trinidad in 1974 when he threw down the stumps after the last ball of the day, running out batsman Alvin Kallicharran who was at that moment blithely on his way back to the pavilion. The West Indies crowd rioted and the run-out decision was reversed when the English team subsequently withdrew their appeal.

Greig said later his action was not premeditated. He'd simply reacted from instinct, not knowing that the game had ended. And you'd believe him, sporting opponents, even sometime critics like Ian Chappell, have nothing but praise for his sportsmanship.

It was bad enough that the Captain of England had signed up to play with some Aussie breakaway outfit, but when the authorities in London found out Greig had been a senior recruiter for WSC – gathering in some of his own team and using his good name to pull in players from the rest of the world, they went feral. Not only was Greig ripped to shreds in the press, but only four days later the Test and County Cricket Board (TCCB) summarily sacked him as England captain, stating 'Greig's action has inevitably impaired the trust which existed between the cricket authorities and the captain of the England side'.

No doubt. It certainly had. And the TCCB's understandable reaction was probably anticipated by Greig and his co-players. The man himself reacted calmly, sticking with standard WSC rhetoric by stating that he'd gone into the whole affair with a view to getting a better deal for cricketers in general. No slouch at PR and with a well-developed understanding of the media, he put himself forward as the man who had sacrificed the greatest jewel in cricket in order to help the 'average' cricketer and to hopefully bring about a better deal for cricket.

But the press wasn't buying it. They went to town on the guy – he was a traitor to the game, a snake in the grass who had acted clandestinely behind the backs of his trusted friends. He wasn't a rebel, he was a sneak, and cricket commentators queued up to take a shot at him. In *The Times* John Woodcock sniffed: 'What has to be remembered, of course, is that he is an Englishman, not by birth or upbringing, but only by adoption. It is not the same thing as being an Englishman through and through'.

Classic stuff, and a beautiful example of what Kerry and his barbarians were up against. Throughout the cricket hostilities the forward-thinking young hot-shots of WSC kept coming up against such nineteenth century puffery. It might have cut it in, say, 1895, but this was the 1970s. As much as anything else, the WSC war was a battle between an antiquated, soon-to-be-fossil-ised world view and the attitudes of a renegade bunch of iconoclasts who saw the revolution clearly. Right at this time the Queen's Silver Jubilee bandwagon was rolling around the British Isles while people like John Wood-cock stood around waving little flags. But The Clash and the Sex Pistols and the Bovver Boys were also out there, choosing to represent a different, and newer, Britain.

Most hurtful to Tony Greig personally was the rev-elation to the world from senior cricket writer Henry Blofeld the following year that Greig was an epileptic. In his book *The Packer Affair* ('A Full Account of the Controversy That Tore Cricket in Two') Blofeld went into bat for the Establishment. 'I have no doubt,' he wrote, 'that if Packer's revolution is successful the ulti-mate loser will be the game of cricket, for the present order of the game will be disrupted and the nature of the game will also change'.

Greig's epilepsy had been an open secret in cricket circles and the clinical reality he shared with, famously, Napoleon, Julius Caesar, Muhammad and Dostoyevski was a part of his life he had learned to control with medication and an understanding of himself and his relationship to the condition. It was something he had not allowed to dominate his daily living. Nevertheless it was a handicap he had chosen for his own reasons not to broadcast, and this was respected by his friends, his sporting peers and the journalists.

Blofeld brought it out into the light by making the spurious point that maybe Greig's condition had in some way impaired his judgment, implying that without epilepsy he might not have taken the crazy step away from the English captaincy into the unknown. It was bullshit of the first order but it exemplifies, more than any other comment, the extent to which the Establishment and its apologists went in badmouthing something they didn't understand.

★

Kerry needed pitches to play on but deafened by the loud sound of cricket ground gates being slammed shut in his face, he went after whatever he could get – the Sydney Showground, home of annual vegetable, live-stock and home-cooking competitions; Gloucester Park in Perth, a harness racing track; and Football Park in Adelaide, centre of South Australia's Australian Rules competition. Top of the list was VFL Park, a massive concrete bunker at Waverley just outside Melbourne, another football venue. But as a backup, John Cornell and Austin Robertson also contracted a cricket ground at St Kilda. Kerry had his sights set on the much larger VFL Park, but sent Cornell and Robertson off to St Kilda anyway. 'The Victorian Football League (VFL) saw cricket as the opposition, so we got St Kilda just in case,' Cornell said, 'I was shocked that Kerry would throw $30,000 at St Kilda "just in case", but if it was going to further his cause, he was good at that.'

Kerry and Cornell choppered out to VFL Park one damp and unpromising May evening to meet Alan Aylett, head of the VFL, a former champion footballer, now a dentist (Aylett became honorary tooth-guy to the WSC players). Shortly after they turned up, the four huge light towers were lit for a VFL game between South Melbourne and Footscray. Kerry and Cornell looked out through the thin night mist at the footballers churning into mud the area where they hoped to play cricket in the coming summer and it didn't help their mood. But the powerful lights held their own magic. Kerry, always with a schoolboy's fascination for the new and the fresh and the untried, gazed around in awe.

'Jesus, son,' he said to Cornell, 'it's almost bright enough to play cricket'.

Not many eureka turning points, in sport or anywhere else, are so clearly defined as this moment. The two men looked at each other, instantly knowing that a flash of insight had passed between them. Perhaps at that second Kerry hadn't grasped the full implication of what he had just said, but Cornell took it that last small step.

He said, 'Hey, that's a good idea, Kerry. Night cricket'.

Bang. Not only was major day-night cricket invented at that moment, but so was the saviour of the whole WSC enterprise. As WSC progressed over the next two years it would be the floodlit matches that the public took to its heart. While other WSC contests languished, struggling to fit with the public's view of what it was trying to achieve, day-night cricket, with its family-oriented informality, its revolutionary white ball and its coloured 'pyjamas' for the players, would come to define WSC in the public imagination.

Cornell and Kerry were in a buoyant mood on their way back to central Melbourne in the chopper. The manifesto for day-night cricket was born on that flight – the two men beginning to realise the full implications of their inspiration.

Night cricket made perfect sense. 'We only play English times,' Cornell recalls their discussion, 'how ridiculous it is, in the heat of the day, we go out and play cricket. We don't even start till eleven. And all around the world in hot countries we're following these old English traditions.' On that return trip above the night lights of Melbourne they came to the conclusion that it was 'a ripper of an idea' and over the following weeks they continued to hone and polish their revelation. Just for starters, night cricket would probably need a different coloured ball to the traditional dark red one. And maybe a few of the game's rules would have to be tweaked – talk to Richie about that. And nights would only work for VFL Park – have to put up lights at other venues. The list went on.

June 1977. Now they were on a roll Kerry decided to muscle up his organisation. He had already been tapping the abilities of CPH executive Lynton Taylor, a smart operator who, as much as anyone could, understood Kerry and had proven himself an exceptional administrator in the family business. Taylor, like Cornell, Greig and Richie Benaud, had a relatively roving brief. Kerry had also recruited former grade cricketer and entrepreneur, Brian Treasure, as administrative controller, and an ex school acquaintance, Christopher Forsyth, as publicity director. *The Great Cricket Hijack,* Forsyth's 1978 record of his adventures as a WSC insider, is dedicated, enigmatically, to 'all those labelled deviant by so-called moral experts who use such labels as acts of power'.

Kerry needed a managing director who could take over the classic supremo position in what was becoming a more complex organisation. After canvassing the views of the others he finally decided on an executive by the name of Vern Stone who was, in a way, already inside the tent. As chief executive of Kerry's Melbourne radio station 3AK Stone had, in four years, lifted it to the top of the Victorian ratings. Kerry got Stone into the office and offered him the job of WSC General Manager. A problem – Stone didn't know much about cricket – he didn't particularly *like* the game. According to Gideon Haigh, this didn't touch Kerry at all.

'Look son', said Kerry, 'you're a young bloke, you're ambitious, you've done a good job. And it suits me that you don't like cricket. Basically I want someone to look after my money and to get this show on the road, because it's one hell of a job.' By all reports Stone took the job reluctantly and probably lived to regret it. As the pressure built, he was the unfortunate point man on many occasions, dealing with deadlines, unforeseen problems and opponents to the whole operation, using diplomacy and executive skills to get the job done – at the same time keeping an eye over his shoulder for the looming presence of Kerry, who wanted it done perfectly, who wanted it done *now* and who didn't want fucking excuses.

Stone hit the ground running. He initially confirmed that the Gabba and the Sydney Cricket Ground (SCG) were running a mile from anything associated with WSC, but managed to sign up the Sydney Showground, Football Park in Adelaide, Gloucester Park in Perth – and grounds in country centres like Orange, Canberra and Geelong for the 'International Country Championship Cup', essentially for the WSC Second XI.

Battle was on, so Kerry called in his troops and the phalanx hit London. Kerry, Cornell, Austin Robertson, Lynton Taylor, Richie Benaud and Kerry's senior *Bulletin* columnist and long-term Packer associate David McNicoll all jetted out of Sydney, heading into enemy territory where the Australia versus England test matches had been raging in a surreal in-between world. The games were still Establishment cricket – a five-test Ashes series – but with a cast of players mostly signed to Kerry. WSC hadn't yet called on their services.

Between matches, Kerry, Cornell and Robertson went off to Brighton to stay with Tony Greig and Donna for a few days. It wasn't a secret, Kerry simply didn't announce his movements, but up until now British reporters had no real idea of who he was or exactly what he was up to. It was a shock for them to find, suddenly, here was The Beast amongst them. Henry Blofeld sniffed him out first.

'A simple piece of espionage enabled us to discover that the large, balding man who arrived in a chauffeur-driven Daimler was Kerry Packer,' he wrote, 'Even seen through the car windows it seemed surprising that he was only forty'.

Blofeld managed to get himself into the 'Captain's Room' at Hove Cricket Ground where Tony Greig was holed up during a Sussex versus Gloucestershire match. Greig introduced him to Kerry, Cornell and Robertson. They all shook hands – Kerry, as Blofeld put it, 'rather limply'.

'I had seen many photographs of him, but even so I was not prepared for quite such an enormous man,' he wrote, 'Every time I have met Packer he has surprised me. On this first occasion, although I never saw him so again, he appeared to be nervous … at times he seemed to be searching for his answers and his later self-assurance had not yet developed.'

He went on, 'Although he said very little, Cornell was the one who appeared in control at that meeting. It was Cornell who had had the original idea, and I suspect that his mind is the most nimble of the three'.

Blofeld asked Kerry what he was doing in the United Kingdom and Kerry's reply was 'watching cricket – which I love'. Asked if he was in the country to talk with the International Cricket Council (ICC), then meeting at Lord's, Kerry said, 'I am prepared to see the relevant cricket authorities at any time they wish to see me, but they have not shown any indication of doing so yet'.

It's probably true that Kerry was, until now, always hoping to compromise with the Establishment, convinced that he could somehow get along with the cricket authorities by simply using his players as leverage. Throughout the saga, like a good cricketer, he kept his eye on the ball – he wanted, firstly, exclusive rights to televise Test cricket in Australia and – now he had the cricketers in his pocket – anything else of value he could finesse from his ownership of them. His bellicose response to the press reaction and the victimisation of Greig was Kerry doing battle – but unlike a lot of people around him, he always knew what the war was all about. Even during the darkest hours he and Tony Greig, who became personally close, hinted at reconciliation at every opportunity. 'I think there's a suggestion in people's minds that we are trying to take over cricket,' he told Blofeld, 'The reason I would like to have talks is to find a solution where we do not have to take over cricket. We don't want to. We would like to see it administered by the traditional authorities. That's why I would like to talk – not to have more influence – but to have less.'

Kerry was also in the United Kingdom to fulfil a promise he had made to David Frost, the pre-eminent TV interviewer of the age, to appear on his television interview show The Frost Report. Standing before a bucolic picket-fenced cricket ground where men in white were in the midst of a game, Frost set the scene: 'Is this peaceful scene, and first-class cricket in general – our national sport – endangered by a new threat from overseas? Cricket – for so many the embodiment of all that is best in the British character, a game in which, until recently, it was the gentlemen that mattered rather than the players. But now a revolutionary new development has come onto the scene. Thirty-five of the best players in the world have been signed up ... not by the traditional authorities but by an independent Australian businessman, Kerry Packer. The result has been official apoplexy.'

In the BBC studio sat Frost, flanked by venerable English cricket legend Jim Laker, Sunday Times cricket columnist Robin Marlar, and Kerry. Throughout the whole half-hour Laker hardly got a word in edgewise

– Marlar went on the attack from the moment the audience's welcoming applause faded. Here was yet another example of an Establishment figure sprouting calcified ideas in the lofty, toffy English tones Australians, and underclass English, instinctively abhor.

'This man doesn't know how to *behave*,' Marlar sniffed, 'He has made Tony Greig do a dishonourable thing'.

When Kerry, who had started out looking visibly nervous, came back with, 'I don't quite understand that'. Marlar quickly interrupted him. 'No you don't,' he said, 'that's just the trouble with you'.

Faced with pomposity and aggressive arrogance, Kerry decided to play a dead bat, sitting calmly beneath the TV arc lights, remaining totally serene as Marlar got visibly heated. The English audience, a mix of men and women, soon chose which side they were on, laughing and jeering at some of Marlar's more risible comments and cheering and applauding Kerry's dry asides.

Marlar: 'This man's intervention is absolutely tearing the guts out of cricket. I fail to see in any way how Mr Packer's intervention is welcome to our cricket here'.

Kerry: 'Well, whether it's welcome here or not there are thirty-five players to start with who want to be in it, and they're the judges. These people have given long service to cricket – they're entitled to a make a decent living out of it'.

Applause from the audience.

Marlar moved on to how he thought it 'a shame' that Tony Greig had lost the English captaincy.

Kerry: 'So do I. But I didn't take it away from him'.

Marlar: 'Well you *did* you see. That's the trouble, you *did*. You *did*'.

Frost: 'How did he take it away?'

Marlar: 'Because, David, here we have a man acting aggressively against an organisation which rightly is not geared up to withstand this kind of business piracy'.

Kerry: 'It's had a hundred years practice. If it's not ready now it'll never be'.

Cheers and applause from the audience.

Marlar: 'No. I'm sorry. I'm sorry to hear people clapping because *this* is the man who does not care about our test cricket'.

Kerry: 'Look, this is about the boards. What I can't understand is their blind reluctance to be informed about what I'm doing, so they can make a balanced decision. Why not talk to me while I'm here?'

Marlar: Because maybe they don't like your attitude. How about that?'

Kerry: 'I think that's highly likely'.

Laughter from the audience.

Marlar: 'David, we still haven't got across the point

that if this circus comes along to—'

Kerry (interrupting): 'It's arrived, boss'.

More audience laughter.

Finally Frost turned to his audience and asked, 'Do you feel the Supertests should go on?' He was greeted with cheering, clapping and cries of 'Yes!'

Frost: 'Or should they be stopped?' Boos. Cries of 'No!' 'No!'

Frost then turned to the camera with, 'Well that seems to be the vote. We'll leave you there. Good night'.

If you were Robin Marlar you'd be convinced you'd just walked into a trap. And you might be right. The partisan crowd gave him a hammering whereas Kerry left the studio with the look of the cat that got the cream. And very recently Frost and Kerry, who were close acquaintances if not friends, had been dancing about each other with a view to Frost appearing on the Nine Network. But it's hard to imagine the BBC going to all the bother of vetting the audience, quizzing them on their views and kicking out anyone who supported the Establishment. The truth is probably that the audience, mostly young people, had a clearer view of what WSC represented than their mothers and fathers of Marlar's age. The danger to the authorities was that this interview had gone out to an audience of millions who had witnessed the unknown Australian businessman being charming, self-deprecating and ironic in the face of stonewalling pomposity. As Blofeld pointed out, 'To most people in Britain Packer's appearance had for the first time put his circus in a sympathetic light'.

Members of the ICC, in front of the TV at home or in their hotel suites, ready for tomorrow's big meeting at Lord's, would have watched with gritted teeth. This big fat Australian was turning into someone it might not be a good idea to go to war with.

★

For 18 days Kerry had sat, pissed off and twiddling his thumbs, in the Dorchester Hotel in Mayfair, waiting for the call-up from the ICC. When it didn't come he took himself away to business meetings in New York. As soon as he left town the ICC sent him a telegram inviting him to meet them at Lord's. It didn't do his mood any good. He insisted they had known all along his date of departure from Heathrow and were just playing some kind of ridiculous war of nerves. But he returned to London happy enough at finally getting his chance to front up to the world's cricket authorities.

On 23 June, a fine, sunny day over London, Kerry, together with Richie Benaud, Lynton Taylor and David

McNicoll arrived at Lord's, climbing out of their limo to be greeted by a bustling horde of reporters and photographers. They made no comment, moved inside and were ushered into the hallowed Lord's Committee Room to face 14 men of the ICC sitting stern around the polished timber board table. It had come down to this moment – Kerry backing himself against the powerful and deeply committed heart of his opposition. He knew if he blew this meeting it was all but over.

After over-formal introductions with forced smiles all round, Kerry was asked by the 67-year-old ICC Chairman William Hugh 'Tagge' Webster if he would like to put his 'proposals' to the assembly. He had heard reports that Mr Packer was open to compromise and he would like to hear what this might represent. Kerry stepped forward and whacked this one back over Webster's head, telling him that in his view a compromise was when two opponents get together, both sides willing to give something so they can move towards each other into some kind of middle ground. He was quite prepared to give a little, but he expected others in the room to do the same.

Fine. Webster now tossed up the five 'conditions' the ICC expected Mr Packer to agree to before any compromise could be reached. They were: that the WSC programs be acceptable to the local cricket authorities and under their control and that the WSC season last not more than six weeks; that no cricketer could play WSC without permission of his local authority; that WSC teams could not be represented as 'national' XIs; that WSC players be made available for Establishment cricket if there was no clash; and that the home authorities be able to honour all their present contracts with sponsors and advertisers.

On the face of them these ultimatums were impossible. The ICC had hit Kerry with five points that in no way looked like compromises. Their effect meant that the ICC kept a tight hold on how cricket would be conducted in the future, despite the fact of the WSC signings. But Kerry chose not to take them head-on. Instead he side-stepped, surprising everyone as, one by one, he agreed to each condition, noting each time that he felt a compromise – an agreed version of the point – might be possible

For 90 minutes an arm-wrestle continued as they debated the points back and forth. Kerry then suggested that a 'working committee' of representatives from both sides could be set up. Webster agreed, smiling, 'Or even two'. Warmth was breaking out all over. Webster now made the point that the ICC having delivered its conditions, would like to know what Mr Packer might be seeking in return.

Thank you very much. Kerry, having all but agreed

to handing his test matches and, by then, 51 of the world's best cricketers back to the ICC, wanted only two things. Firstly, that the ICC guarantee that his players would not be victimised in the way Tony Greig had been by getting stripped of his captaincy of England, and secondly the TV rights to future Test series in Australia after the ABC's contract expired. He made it clear he was willing to pay a lot of money for those rights, that he didn't expect to be given them.

Chris Forsyth says Kerry looked around at the 14 stern faces gazing at him in studied concentration. He waited … then cut through the long silence, saying, 'Gentlemen, would you like us to step outside while you discuss that? We'll just have a look around while you chat'.

The four Australians went outside into the fine sunshine and strolled about the hallowed wicket of the sacred ground. Their discussion centred on whether the delegates would accept what Kerry had put to them. Kerry was buoyant, gazing around in awe at the famous sloping ground, convinced that the fight was just about over. Upstairs, inside, it was a different story. Bob Parish and Ray Steele of the ACB were briefing the delegates on their meeting with Kerry back in June, how they had a longstanding and functioning TV relationship with the ABC, how they had informed Kerry of this, how they had told him to go away until 1979, at which time he could bid for the rights along with everyone else. The discussion went on for 40 minutes. Then Kerry was called back in...

He would have known the moment he stepped into the room that his day had turned to dust and bitter ashes. The faces of the 14 would have told him. He's quoted as saying, 'before our seats were warm in the bloody chairs' Webster read out two short lines, stating that it was the unanimous decision of the member countries of the ICC that exclusive television rights could not be granted in advance. 'Will you agree to that?' said Webster.

'No sir,' said Kerry.

'Then I'm afraid there is nothing further to discuss,' said Webster.

The meeting lasted a total of two and a quarter hours. Kerry, frustrated, furious, left the conference room, strode down the corridor and stepped out into the sun where he ploughed into the jostling media scrum. 'I am only in the arena because of my disagreement with the Australian Cricket Board', he snarled, 'Had I got those TV rights I was prepared to withdraw from the scene and leave the running of cricket to the Board. I will not take steps to help anyone. It's every man for himself and the devil take the hindmost'.

Both sides had settled their positions and dug their trenches. From now on it would be total war.

2
CONFLICT

Led by his obstreperous nature, it seems Kerry's instinctive reaction to any setback was always to plunge on angrily, bursting across the room kicking furniture out of the way like Liberty Valance. It was one of his greatest virtues, this tough, take-no-prisoners attitude to anyone he thought might have been trying to dominate him. Having been bullied by his father for 35 years, the now 40-year-old was finding new ways to rid himself of the bitter inheritance by turning himself into the supreme bullying bastard-guy. His peers and those who worked closely with him in the 1970s attest to his ability to tear into anyone who displeased him with an absolutely terrifying – and mostly unjustified – ferocity. And those closest to him copped it most. One senior executive, describing him as 'a mean bugger', recalls how Kerry terrified his dedicated and highly effective long-term private secretary Pat Wheatley to such an extent that she took to keeping a bottle of scotch under her desk to calm her nerves.

As Chris Forsyth has pointed out, the unpredictability of Kerry's moods made dealing with him akin to 'handling the ends of a broken power cable with the current turned on'. 'His moods slide up and down according to the tempo of the day,' he wrote, 'He is at his worst when the outlook is murky and he cannot perceive the way ahead; or when the situation requires a change of plans. In this way he is inflexible and jittery. An extraordinary and unexpected transformation occurs and the cool commercial Packer, the ratings-orientated shot-calling media magnate becomes a ferocious, cruel, shouting tyrant, incapable of distinguishing between what is important and what is not'.

By all accounts Kerry used his size – he was 6 feet, 1 inch tall and 18 stone – and loud, wharfie language to intimidate anyone who came into his orbit. WSC cricketers and CPH executives, interviewed about the man, lapse into loud Kerry talk, enjoying playing him like actors as they quote him. They puff out their chests, lower their voices in tone, raise them in volume and start spouting Kerryisms. Ian Chappell, discussing his recruitment into WSC grinned, raised his voice and, taking Kerry off, gave it this way: 'What do you think this is, a *fucking* democracy? I'm *fucking* paying the bills. I'll *fucking* pick the captain. You're the *fucking* captain. Now who do you want on the *fucking* team?' Others do the same. Kerry probably didn't swear quite as much as these guys recall, what sticks in their memories is Kerry dropping 'fuck' into his speech as some kind of verbal support for aggression. It was conscious tactical policy on Kerry's part. Ita Buttrose insists Kerry, the well-brought-up young man, well-versed in 1950s courtesy and good manners, never swore in front of women.

Well brought up by a brutish role-model father at home, so the bullying extended to family. Part of the whole WSC deal was that Kerry would put $200,000 into a scheme for cricket coaching of schoolchildren. The top young players would be helped out by Kerry's champions at various grounds in the state capitals, even in the country centres and sometimes at their schools. One bright Sunday, Kerry ordered his West Indian players to turn up to his son James' school Cranbrook, an expensive private school in Sydney's Eastern Suburbs, to coach the First XI. Ten-year-old James, by all accounts a gently singular kid, who used to practice batting against a bowling machine in the backyard at home in Bellevue Hill, tagged along with Dad to see his West Indian heroes. They watched the 18-year-old batsmen of the school's First XI doing their utmost against lollypops tossed up by Joel Garner, Andy Roberts and Michael Holding. Then Kerry stepped forward and told James to get his bat and go to the crease. James declined. Kerry's jaw tightened. He turned to a Channel 9 cameraman, on the spot filming for a documentary, told him to put his camera away then ordered James to get to the crease and 'be a man'. James stepped up bravely.

As a scattering of West Indies players and the documentary crew looked on the fast bowlers lobbed a few light tosses to the little boy who managed to pat them away. Kerry stepped in again and ordered them to bowl faster, so James copped a few at about half pace, each ball whipping past him faster than anything the home bowling machine was ever capable of. 'No. Bowl at him full pace,' said Kerry. The guys refused – hey come on man...

Kerry glared. 'You bloody well will. Do it.' The threat was there so, obviously using everything in their armoury to fool Kerry, they let fly at the now quivering kid. Kerry watched the ten-year-old cop a few terrifying moments before calling a halt and wandering away from the embarrassed onlookers and his sobbing son.

Ita Buttrose tells how even when his father was still alive, the staff and everyone else round the Consolidated Press building in Sydney's Park Street would avoid Kerry on the days that he had his 'Mogadon headaches'. A lifetime insomniac, Kerry would take Mogadon to try to knock himself out, be awake all night then have to go into work. He would throw phones, staplers, files, anything he could lay his hands on, at hapless staffers, but this was spur-of-the moment stuff which he described as something merely to 'keep them on their toes'.

Kerry would sometimes call the heads of WSC departments into his office (he had a switchboard console at his desk that could cut into the phone conversations of his executives) and get stuck into them one at a time. With a cigarette between his fingers and often another one burning in an ashtray, he'd point an accusing finger – 'What the fuck have you been doing lately? Sitting on your arse probably. Get the *fuck* out of here and get it done!' During WSC, Richie Benaud and John Cornell were the only two who were spared this indignity and humiliation. The venomous finger would move up and over them and onto the next hapless victim.

Chris Forsyth recalls attending one particular WSC meeting where Kerry decided to victimise one of his senior operatives, administrative controller Brian Treasure. After beating him up for much of the meeting, Kerry, on his way out to go and attend court, pointed the dreaded finger at Treasure: ' "I'm going to court now," growls Packer, "I'm going to straighten out what you fouled up." He stares a moment longer at Treasure, whirls and stalks out the door. The dying rasp of his voice echoes through the room. Treasure cannot believe what has happened. His expression is bewildered, hurt. "But it wasn't me – it wasn't my fault," insists Treasure. Finding Packer out of earshot he turns to face us and repeats more softly, "It wasn't my fault".

For a moment he stands; a forlorn figure needing a friend, trying to convince us, and meets only embarrassment, sympathy, curiosity, contempt or neutralism in our stares.'

The guys in the room are feeling for Treasure, but their dominant thought would have been, 'At least it wasn't me'. We witness the other prisoners being tortured and beaten, we see the blood on the batons, and we think there but for the Grace of God...

★

Kerry's 'devil take the hindmost' outburst on the front steps of Lord's on 23 June 1977 might have been typical, but it was dumb. He kicked up a whole new wasps' nest of hostility and unnecessary opposition. Immediately the press picked up on his 'I am only in the arena because of my disagreement with the Australian Cricket Board'. Aha! they said, what about all his guff about helping cricketers? He and Tony Greig have been banging on about the reasons behind the rebel group being somehow altruistic and how cricketers have been getting a rough trot from the authorities – now that's revealed as bullshit. All along, this guy's only been in it to make money from TV. And Kerry only compounded his problem when, the following day, quizzed by a journalist about his TV ambitions, he leisurely replied, 'That was the reason that we got into it from the beginning'.

A second wave of aggressively bad press now followed, best put by E.W. Swanton in *The Cricketer International*. Kerry had, he wrote, 'emerged in his true colours ... so much for the protestations that he had gone into cricket to improve the lot of the downtrodden first-class cricketer!' Swanton went on to describe the players as nothing more than 'pawns in a local commercial dog-fight'.

It was a reasonable charge. But the two points of view, Kerry's and that of the Establishment commentators like Swanton were not mutually exclusive. Having stated his commercial interests, Kerry's rhetoric continued to be all about how he would never abandon his players, how he would fight to make sure they were well paid now and into the future, and how he was powerfully opposed to the cricket authorities trying to punish or victimise them in any way. In his mind, the money and the cricketers were two sides of the same coin – chicken and egg. Now they were signed up to him he would use all his power to protect them and lead them to a better future – but there was no way on earth he was going to lose money on the deal.

The boss's truculent posturing posed a problem for those on the payroll whose job it was to clean up after him – most notably his number one diplomat and strategist, Richie Benaud. It has gone down in cricketing lore how Benaud, throughout the whole tussle, would urge Kerry to 'make love, not war'. The genesis of this came in a memo Benaud whipped off to Lynton Taylor immediately after Kerry's outburst:

> Please, when you get back to Australia start
> making love not war. The press has been
> desperately bad from the public relations point of
> view over that statement and the devil bit. As it
> is our job to pick up the pieces, I'd like to think a
> more gentle approach could be evolved. With that
> statement already made, cricket authorities have
> gained a great deal by way of sympathy.

Kerry didn't improve things when, in the same fit of pique, he announced he had earlier been willing to play his games on dates that did not clash with official Test matches, in the hope that some sort of deal could be done, but because of the ICC's intransigence he would now schedule his looming Supertests on the exact days of that summer's official Test matches. None of his players would be available to the Establishment, no matter what.

The energised press now hit Tony Greig with its second wave. He was still seen as a traitor to English cricket, independent of any debate going on about money or TV rights. Bored journalists on a slow day would take another whack at him just for something to do, and the cricketing public, so fond of him just weeks ago, took to catcalling and booing every time he walked onto a cricket field. Kerry's appearance in the United Kingdom at this time was partly to take the heat off Greig, but it didn't help much.

John Crilly had been a talented TV director, working closely with John Cornell on the Hogan show and various sports series for Channel 9. Cornell recruited him to WSC and Crilly headed off to Britain with his film crew to check out the scene and shoot some footage for future promos. They arrived at Hove Cricket Ground to speak to Tony Greig and were let in for free. Crilly chatted with Greig then watched the man copping insults from the crowd as he went out to bat. He'd been witnessed talking to the most hated man in England – so when he left the ground he and his crew were charged £30 by the same official.

A leading light in WSC, a friend of Kerry's and genuinely convinced of the legitimacy of the whole venture,

Greig stood up well under the barrage, but in July 1978 the moment came that altered his view. The attack came home to his family. At his young daughter Samantha's school it was the norm for the teacher to hand out kids' birthday party invitations to every member of the class. On a day that Greig was there to pick up Samantha, her best friend's birthday invitations were being handed round. Samantha stood waiting eagerly for her invitation but there wasn't one for her. Samantha's best friend rushed to her mother to tell her of the mistake. In Samantha's hearing the mother told her daughter, 'She's not invited'.

'I took three strides towards Samantha, who jumped into my arms, tears running down her face,' Greig wrote later, 'I would not have minded if that woman had said to my face that she did not agree with what I had done to cricket … but to take out her feelings on two tiny, unsuspecting girls was surely unforgiveable. I felt physically sick, and from that moment on my life in England was finished.' The family later moved to Sydney.

After the 23 June meeting there was an eerie silence from the ICC as its associated world bodies retired to their various foxholes to decide on the next move. Huddled in a deafening silence, telegrams and international phone calls whizzing round the globe, they were clearly about to come up with some kind of spectacular killer blow. Back in Sydney, Kerry, wondering what the hell they were up to, held a press conference where he rattled sabres and made vague aggressive threats. But there was nothing to be done until they showed their hand, so while they plotted, he simply got on with the job – he and his troops had quite a bit to go on with if they were to stage a whole season of five-day and one-day cricket matches starting in Australia in the coming summer.

Crucial amongst the legal, budgeting, tax, marketing, advertising, accommodation and travel problems, were the pitches – the all-important playing surfaces. Richie Benaud is reported as saying, 'The wickets will be the first thing we're judged on – if they're lacking the whole thing could go down the drain'.

A not unexpected blow came in July 1977 when the SCG Trust turned down WSC's application to play on the SCG, considered one of the world's great cricket grounds. Trust Chairman Pat Hills announced that the ground was held by the Trust in a long-term arrangement with the NSW Cricket Association and WSC would not be allowed anywhere near the place. Kerry would have expected this, nevertheless, keeping to his theme of painting his opposition as yesterday's men, he told the press the decision was made by 'a group of crusty old men sitting behind closed doors'.

The search for playing fields was on. The whole enterprise was, at its core, based on athletes who played on strips of soil and grass that for the past hundred years had been carefully tended by groundsmen who understood the dark and mysterious art of making a length of dirt that could be torn apart by bats, fast balls and sprigged shoes for five days without collapsing altogether. The wicket, the cricketers will tell you, is the critical element that decides whether you will play your fast bowlers or your spinners, whether you bat first or put the other guy in, even who you choose in your final XI. Over five days, a thousand tiny decisions have to be made according to how well or badly groundsmen have laid, sown, rolled, watered and mowed. No other gladiatorial game in the world is so intrinsically, intimately, caught up with micro-agriculture. In mid 1977 the only grounds Kerry could find were fleapit football fields, at their centre stressed, muddy and broken by hundreds of boots churning them into mush. It was now late autumn in Australia and even if there weren't footballers all over the contracted WSC grounds, there simply wasn't enough time to plant grass and have it mowable, rollable and tough enough to play on by November. Lawn grass just doesn't grow in winter. Turning any of the ovals into a decent surface for first-class cricket in half a growing season was an impossibility.

Enter John Maley, the 30-year-old groundsman at Brisbane's Woollongabba cricket field, a soil expert and the man described by Henry Blofeld as 'perhaps the main hero of the Packer revolution'. After being recommended by Greg Chappell, Maley joined up and in April was given the impossible task of getting the wickets ready. Luckily Maley, a lean and bearded wry wicket genius, was the only person who knew the impossible was achievable. He and everyone else knew there was no way on earth a conventional wicket could be grown on the grounds where one didn't already exist, so he came up with the idea of building them elsewhere from scratch.

'Working from a small unpretentious caravan which served as a laboratory, administrative office, operations centre, telephone exchange, kitchen, dining room and sometime bedroom, parked on the gravel road beside the hothouse at Waverley, Maley did something which no other curator of his time ever thought of doing,' wrote Chris Forsyth.

What he thought of doing was carting specially sourced soil into hothouses where he had huge 25-tonne concrete trays, drainage pipes at the bottom, with a layer of gravel followed by sand, then lines of warming cables covered by loam, topped by black clay soil, all laid out under special lights. It sounds like a description of haute cuisine. And it worked. Maley and his team carefully tended the couch grass they planted in the trays, watering, fertilising, giving it the perfect night and day temperature conditions to nurse it into life. The grass grew like crazy and soon the massive trays were ready to be trucked out to the various grounds and put into place.

Here was a problem. The 25-tonnes of tray and soil, each one half a cricket pitch long (they joined at the centre), would take some mammoth equipment to wrangle into the middle of the grounds, but the weight of any industrial cranes and low loaders would damage the playing surface of the ground, seriously rutting the outfield. A eureka moment arrived. What about we get hovercraft to float the things into place? The idea was just crazy enough to work. The plan was to fit a tight rubber skirt round the edges of the trays and pump air into the whole thing. It'd then lift off the ground, purely on air pressure, and float gently out to the centre to be lowered into place. Piece of piss.

Unfortunately – surprise – it didn't work. Kerry was there to witness the fiasco and was understandably displeased. Success has a thousand fathers but failure is an orphan. It's impossible to pin down with any certainty whose plan this actually was – even after all these years they're still running a mile.

But time was of the essence, the wickets *had* to be in place. Vern Stone found some big-ticket movers who said they could do the job – for just under $20,000 – by laying metal plates out on the field to protect it then slowly rolling the trays out to the centre on low-loaders before swinging them into place with cranes. The hover-craft would have been 50 per cent cheaper, but at least this method worked. WSC had another critical element firmly in place. Maley's wickets were a triumph.

This was the sharp end of the preparations for the looming WSC summer. Things were beginning to fall into place – or at least be forced into place by John Cornell who had, in Gideon Haigh's words 'a myste-rious mission as floating creative catalyst', plus Richie and Daphne Benaud and their team, Austin Robert-son, Lynton Taylor, Vern Stone, Brian Treasure and the others, all working 16-hour days. Executive Producer for the upcoming TV telecasts, David Hill and his direc-tors Brian Morelli and John Crilly – in the first year these two shared directing duties before Morelli took over fulltime – their technical manager Warren Berkery and chief sound guy Colin Stevenson were out at the grounds with their cameras and sound equipment, making it up as they went along, inventing what would soon become the standard form of televising not only cricket but almost every other sport.

Hill, who had been recruited from HSV-7 in Melbourne, began with the traditional single end camera – the calcified set up beloved by the ABC and BBC since television first arrived at cricket grounds. But he knew his brief was to go beyond that, mainly from Kerry's immortal line to him at a meeting, 'I don't want to fucking spend half a game looking at the fucking batsman's arse'.

At first Hill and his directors Crilly and Morelli blew the concept wide open by doubling it – what about cameras at both ends? So far so good. After that 'the coverage evolved,' says Hill, 'It was a day-by-day thing. Let's try this, let's put that there and see what happens.' If two cameras, why not three ... or four? Hell, why not fucking *six*? They positioned a 'follow' camera at each end with trained cameramen who expertly followed the ball, a side slips camera at each end, a mid-wicket camera and a wide-shot camera up in the commentary box. The arithmetic addition of each single camera made the coverage geometrically more difficult, Morelli and Crilly, talented directors, were on a steep learning curve and so were their cameramen. Then came another idea – let's have a down and dirty roving camera on the sidelines. Their 'field hand-held' filming brought cricket into living rooms with an immediacy sport had never before experienced. At their peak Morelli and Crilly were dealing with nine cameras.

John Cornell is credited with the initial idea of wicket microphones, tiny mikes set into the ground at each end to record the thoughts and feelings of the batsmen and often the wicketkeepers and slips fielders as well. It meant laying a thin cable in a trench all the way across the field to the centre and tucking it down near the wicket. Problem: what if it rains? The microphone'll be ruined. Solution: slip the thing into a condom. Now the mikes might've been waterproof but they weren't cricketer proof. 'The cricketers, God bless them, thought it a great lark to stomp all over the mikes and break them,' said Hill. So he and outside broadcast manager Warren Berkery got together 'over a few beers' and worked out they could get a much better result by hollowing out a stump and setting a battery-powered radio microphone inside.

Cricket was now lit, shot from every possible angle and wired for sound. Word had been filtering out of the technical innovations going on in Sydney and Melbourne. Asked about it in London, BBC's Head of Sport, Jonathon Martin declared the BBC would never change its cricket coverage, 'until hell freezes over'. But only a short time later the BBC, along with every other cricket-coverage network in the world was emulating the WSC innovations. 'The day they did that I called Jonathon and inquired if it was a tad chilly in his office,' says Hill. In three years WSC changed the face of cricket coverage forever.

★

Meanwhile Kerry, at the centre of the vortex, was playing his strategic game with the Establishment, thinking the big picture while the rest got on with making it all work. By now he had completed his plunder of the world's cricketers. He was playing with a full deck while the cricket authorities, he said, were busy with their 'third eleven'. With a few more signings and pickups, in November 1977 these are the players he had ready to go into battle.

The Australians – Ian Chappell, Greg Chappell, Ray Bright, Trevor Chappell, Ian Davis, Ross Edwards, Gary Gilmour, David Hookes, Martin Kent, Bruce Laird, Rob Langer, Dennis Lillee, Ashley Mallett, Mick Malone, Rodney Marsh, Rick McCosker, Graham McKenzie, Kerry O'Keefe, Len Pascoe, Wayne Prior, Ian Redpath, Richie Robinson, Max Walker, Doug Walters.

The West Indians – Clive Lloyd, Deryck Murray,

Jim Allen, Wayne Daniel, Roy Fredericks, Joel Garner, Gordon Greenidge, Michael Holding, David Holford, Bernard Julien, Collis King, Albert Padmore, Vivian Richards, Andy Roberts, Lawrence Rowe.

The World – Tony Greig (England), Zaheer Abbas (Pakistan), Dennis Amiss (England), Eddie Barlow (South Africa), Asif Iqbal (Pakistan), Imran Khan (Pakistan), Majid Khan (Pakistan), Alan Knott (England), Mushtaq Mohammad (Pakistan), Mike Procter (South Africa), Barry Richards (South Africa), John Snow (England), Derek Underwood (England), Bob Woolmer (England).

Timeless champions. Kerry had managed to pick the jewels out of the cricket crown.

It's an interesting fact that there were no Indian players in the rebel troupe. Seven Indian players were approached, including renowned batsman Sunil Gavaskar and ace spin bowler Bishan Bedi. By all reports Gavaskar and some of the others were willing to sign up but Bedi, a strong traditionalist and the Indian captain of the moment, managed to convince them it was not a good idea.

All up, in the coming Australian summer, the players would be involved in 88 days' cricket played on 17 different grounds. With a surfeit of cricketers the plan was to have a two-tier competition. The Australians, the

West Indians and the World side would play six Super-tests and a series of one-day matches for the International Cup in the capital cities. Then there was a series of two- and three-day games for the International Country Championship Cup, played in country towns by whoever didn't make it to the First XIs. To administer this facet of the outfit Kerry signed up 36-year-old businessman John Curtain, a graduate of the London School of Economics, as assistant manager (Administration) who zipped around the country centres arranging for the circus to come to town. The Country Championship players, used to being considered the cream of the game, bristled at playing as the Second XI. But you could make your way out of Rockhampton and into Melbourne if you played well enough. Ian Chappell, captaining the top Australian team, always kept a weather eye out on the form of the guys in country matches.

Meanwhile in England, the Australian Test team, made up mostly of WSC signatories but still without Lillee, was getting thrashed by the English team, led by its new skipper Mike Brearley, a Cambridge-educated, academically inclined batsman who could also keep wicket. Thirty-five year old Brearley actually looked the part. Tall and lean, at the wicket with a bat in his hand he stood stiffly erect, looking for all the world like some aristocratic Country Life batsman from two generations earlier – the perfect image the cricket Establishment was trying to convey.

Brearley was a decent captain who might have looked the stereotype but, like the very best of English captains, loved pounding Australians into the dirt – which he did very effectively. He had his own view of the breakaway rebels and their impact on cricket, choosing an intelligently objective approach to the whole business. At no point did he publicly condemn Greig for his actions, as a matter of fact he attacked the 'hysterical accusations' made against his predecessor and gracefully noted that he would have considered joining WSC if he had been invited. When, after one Test match, a £9000 bonus was to be paid to the English players, despite quite a bit of opposition he insisted that the WSC signatories in his team, Tony Greig, Derek Underwood and Alan Knott share in the spoils along with everyone else.

Led by Greg Chappell the Australians played the usual bunch of minor games, three one-day internationals and five full Test matches – losing for a lot of the time. There's no way of telling whether the uncertainty of the moment had a hand in Australia's dismal performance, but you'd put money on their minds not being fully on the job. The coming Australian summer of 1977–78 would make or break their whole careers, and there was this terrible silence from Lord's, which implied that something nasty was about to come down. And some of the team had been signed to WSC, some not – a recipe for trouble. Rumours spread of frayed nerves and unrest within the Australian camp, so tour manager Len Maddocks issued a press release denying that the guys' performance was in any way affected by the cricket politics swirling about their heads:

> I understand that there have been rumours
> spreading to the effect that there is unrest in the
> Australian team, mainly because some players are
> signed to play with the Kerry Packer organisation
> while others are not. The players unanimously
> have asked me to state that this is not the case.

It might not have been the case, but *something* was out of kilter. The Ashes were a disaster – two games were drawn and England won the other three. The Australians didn't win a Test.

★

Kerry and his administrators and players were braced for attack – and they weren't disappointed. At the end of July 1977, the ICC came roaring out of its huddle at Lord's. ICC Secretary Jack Bailey issued a statement confirming that the ICC member countries were convinced that 'the whole structure of cricket' was under threat and that cricket itself would be 'severely damaged' if the WSC games went ahead. And just to confirm the ICC's old-school disposition the whole statement was worded in archaic legalese that had journalists chuckling as they typed it into their articles.

> Notwithstanding anything hereinbefore contained,
> 'it said', no player who after October 1 1977
> has made himself available to play in a match
> previously disapproved by the Conference shall
> thereafter be eligible to play in any Test match
> without the express consent of the Conference to
> be given only on the application of the governing
> body for cricket of the country for which but for
> this sub-rule the player would be eligible to play.
> … and so on.

Naming itself as the 'sole promoter' of cricket, the ICC in essence gave the players until the first of October to renege on their agreements with Kerry or be banned from ever playing international cricket. Most of the press put this down as the death-knell for WSC, figuring that, now presented with the stark choice, the players would rather play for their countries than for any rebel 'exhibition' matches – as the ICC referred to them. There was that 'exhibition' problem again. The ICC and those journalists predicting the demise of World Series because of a wave of players' defections didn't quite get that the cricketers saw WSC cricket as something else entirely.

To add to the pressure, the ICC went on to say any rebel matches that did go ahead, even though played by the best of the world's cricketers, would not be considered 'First Class' and the scores would never be entered into the official record books. (To this day WSC's 56,126 runs and 2364 wickets go unrecognised and unacknowledged by the ICC and WSC statistics are not to be found in Wisden.) Any player who decided to kick on and play for WSC would be 'disapproved', the ICC said, and just to ram it home, any match organised by Kerry and Richie Benaud or any other 'associated companies or persons' was also 'disapproved'. By naming these two men the ICC officially made them 'disapproved persons', a move that reportedly hit Benaud hard. The man who had spent his whole life in the service of cricket and had done so much for the game found himself all but excluded by the world's top decision-making body.

And the squeeze continued. The English Test and County Cricket Board (TCCB) was due to meet in

September when it would ban all the English WSC players from playing county cricket, and the Australian Cricket Board was set to do the same with the 24 Australians, banning them from state Sheffield Shield cricket. They might even be banned from playing grade and district games. The other countries – the West Indies authorities were not fully convinced but not rocking the boat – would follow suit. The ban was blanket and complete.

Kerry came back in an uncharacteristically calm and stoic manner, stating that the ICC decision was regrettable but 'predictable'. He said the players had always known this was a distinct possibility from the outset and had chosen to go ahead anyway. He had been in contact with his cricketers and none of them had changed their minds, in fact they were more strongly resolved than ever to make his 'Supertests' and one-dayers work. He could afford to be calm and must have been smiling a little inside. No doubt he had anticipated this exact move, but he also knew the ICC, in one show, had played its whole hand. They had nothing more to fight with. He could now get on with the war with his enemy clearly in his sights knowing they had nothing nasty up their sleeve, knowing if his 51 champions kept their nerve official Test cricket would from now on be played by the reserves. And the cricket public would soon be voting.

He was also buoyed by the fact that the NSW Government, led by Premier Neville Wran had, that very day, sacked all 13 members of the SCG Trust which had refused WSC use of its iconic ground, and replaced them with a fresh 12-man board that was expected to give Kerry the green light in quick time. There was quite a bit of screaming and tut-tutting in various quarters – how come, only 24 hours after they say no to Packer, the whole Trust gets the heave-ho? To say it was a controversial decision is to understate it. But the NSW Government, hand over its heart, declared it a 'coincidence'. Kerry immediately resubmitted his offer to use the ground. Problem fixed.

★

But despite Kerry's sanguine demeanour the ICC's attack bit into parts of the WSC body and prompted others to do the same. Just 48 hours after the ICC bombshell Australian David Lord, fast bowler Jeff Thomson's agent, announced that Thomson was withdrawing from WSC. In his youth Lord had been a grade cricketer. He was now a journalist, cricket writer and burgeoning agent. Thomson fronted the press on the morning of 28 July and told the assembled hacks, 'I'm tearing up my contract'.

Somehow it had slipped his mind that when he signed with WSC he already had a pre-existing and watertight contract with Brisbane radio station 4IP. Chris Forsyth quotes him that day: 'I was with a bunch of lads at the time and it seemed OK and I signed. I did not think it would breach my contract with 4IP and I was told it would not interfere with my cricket career. But it has, so I have withdrawn'.

Three days later another Lord client, West Indian wicketkeeper Alvin Kallicharran, announced that he too was tearing up his contract, joining 4IP and playing cricket for Queensland. Nervous WSC cricketers started checking with lawyer mates to see if they too could join in if there was a rush for the doors. Rumours flew, and leading the rumour-mill was the word that top West Indian batsman Viv Richards – another in Lord's stable – plus Thomson's good mate Australian batsman Len Pascoe, were also about to jump. To make matters worse, back in Adelaide a group of anti-WSC businessmen had tipped in to a 'Keep Hooksey At Home' fund. The plan was to get as close as possible to his WSC money, at the same time appealing to Hookes' parochialism. He would return to playing for South Australia and, by extension, Australia. The captaincy of both were dangled in front of him – hard to resist for a 22-year-old with a long and hopefully distinguished career ahead.

David Lord saw it all clearly: 'I think this will be the beginning of the exodus from the Packer circus,' he said, and in the *Daily Telegraph* he couldn't resist taking further swipes at Kerry:

I am tickled pink because at last some sanity
has prevailed ... I will now be putting the same
pressure on my other players because, frankly,
I have been waiting for the moment to break
Packer ... The players themselves have just
followed each other like sheep without thinking
about it. But suddenly they have had an attack of
the brains.

Kerry got all this news from the United Kingdom at home in Sydney. He immediately did two things: he got his best lawyers to go over the cricketers' contracts to see if there were any loopholes big enough for his players to bolt through, and he leapt on a plane to London to see if he could steady his ship. With all the whispering and rumours flying around, who knows what was going on within the ranks of his players – he needed to stiffen their resolve before things got out of hand. Before taking off he's reported to have phoned Kallicharran and threatened to sue. Meetings with lawyers were set up, threats were made, Kallicharran copped the full Kerry blast, but in the end it all petered out and Kerry, who after blustering about and threatening to leave Thomson and Kallicharran 'barefoot and bankrupt', decided not to chase them.

In London, in his suite in the Dorchester, he held a summit conference with his top advisers and a brace of lawyers and although they left the cricketers alone they took after Lord with a heavy club. Lord was sued for allegedly wrongfully pressuring Jeff Thomson and Alvin Kallicharran to renege on their WSC contracts. WSC sought an injunction stopping him from inducing anyone else from doing the same. In the end Viv Richards and Len Pascoe stayed inside the tent, but David Lord continued as the targeted enemy of WSC. John Cornell describes Lord's professed declaration to 'break' Kerry as nothing more than 'a fit of ego-driven mania'.

Kerry now settled his troops, calling them together in his Dorchester suite and turning on drinks and a fine spread. He was aware of the 'Keep Hooksey At Home' movement in Adelaide and the fact that some of the guys were genuinely apprehensive. Senior players like Ian Chappell, Tony Greig and Dennis Lillee, who had been on the inside from the genesis and who had close contact with Kerry, had none of the jitters of the younger players who saw that if things went severely wrong their fresh, promising careers would come crashing to a premature and ignominious close.

As they sipped nervously at their beers – many of them had never met him – Kerry moved amongst them in the luxurious suite and used the sheer power of his overwhelming presence to get promises of fidelity one-by-one. Gideon Haigh reports Kerry circled the room 'eyeing each individual ... "Is anyone here having second thoughts? Is there anyone who thinks what they're saying is right, that you're a 'disapproved person'?" Each player was fronted. "Are you in?" Each assented.' Australian batsman Ian Davis is quoted as saying that after Kerry's magisterial performance, 'I think it put me back on the path to World Series. After that I just thought "I'm committed, I'll stick with it".' Mick Malone said, 'Packer's physical presence was awesome. And because he was so direct and forthright, he came across as a powerful individual whose side you wanted to be on.' Even David Hookes gave Kerry the nervous nod. 'The Boss' had managed to put out a major bushfire.

★

Kerry's major counter-attack to the ICC's ban was more court action – a move that many media commentators and cricket followers had anticipated. It was decided that Tony Greig, John Snow and Mike Proctor would be the plaintiffs in a High Court case against the ICC and the TCCB, charging that the bans constituted 'restraint of trade' and an inducement to the cricketers to break their contracts with the Packer outfit. The WSC claim was that the authorities' actions were unconscionable and contrary to the law because they unfairly prevented the cricketers from plying their trade – playing cricket – depriving them of the ability to earn a living in the only way they knew how. Kerry hired the services of brilliant English QC Robert Scott Alexander, a big man with a fearsome reputation in British legal circles. Alexander was a cricket-lover and longstanding member of the Marylebone Cricket Club – the fabled MCC – but without any of the reactionary toff about him.

Kerry's recruitment of Alexander, the pre-eminent silk of his day who later became Baron Alexander of Weedon, and described as the finest barrister of his generation, has gone down in legend and is another example of Kerry enjoying who he was and the power that came with it. Jock Harper, one of Kerry's legal brains in the Australian law firm, Allen Allen & Hemsley, arranged for Kerry to meet up with the London solicitors, Linklaters & Paines, to discuss the retaining of a barrister. The day of the appointment came through, but on that day Kerry, Tony Greig and Jock Harper were due to be choppered out of London to go and play golf. No problem, they just called in and said they'd be in golf clothing for the meeting.

'So off we go in our golf gear,' says Greig, 'We wait, and these guys come in. I'll never forget it. There was this row of pinstripe suits, looking every part the English barrister establishment.'

Kerry, looking forward to his golf day, was keen to get this over and done with. 'He was in a bit of a ballsy mood' says Greig. 'He said, "We don't want this thing to go on for too long, we've got to get on the golf course".'

Kerry, Greig and Harper found themselves sitting opposite half a dozen sombre, eminent pinstriped solicitors, drinking coffee out of tiny demitasses and listening to the well-rounded vowels of some introductory chit-chat. Kerry listened to this for a short time before interrupting. 'Hang on', he said, 'as you can see, we haven't got much time. Can I ask you blokes first of all, who's the best QC in the land'.

After a bit of tut-tutting back came the elegant reply that, ahh… perhaps it was different in Australia, but Britain had a great many eminent silks and the fellows in the room would be most happy to select one for Mr Packer. The atmosphere in the room changed at that moment.

'At this point I can see Kerry's just starting to boil.

And I'm thinking, Oh God, if only you knew this bloke,' says Greig.

'Perhaps you didn't hear the question,' Kerry said calmly, 'who's the best QC in the country?' Back came more of the same. 'Mr Packer, please, it's rather a complex process, you must leave this to us. It's a question of availability. And the *cost*.'

'Well,' says Greig, 'Kerry just blew up. He said, "Jock we're wasting our time here. I'm going to play golf. May I suggest you have a talk to these guys and tell them how we work. And it might just be a good fuckin' idea to tell them we're not scared of the expense".'

Kerry walked out of the room. He and Greig went off and played a most enjoyable 18 holes.

A few days later they returned, walking into the room to find there had been a subtle change – the pin-striped solicitors had brought in an extra player, there were now seven. This time when his little demitasse of coffee arrived Kerry waved it away and before any chit-chat could start, eyed the row of men and said, 'Right. Do you guys remember the question?'

This time they were most eager to please. 'Mr Packer, we've narrowed it down to three.'

'A step in the right direction,' says Kerry, 'Narrowed down from a cast of thousands to three. So who are they?'

The head pinstriped guy started the list: 'Right, first there's Mr Robert Alexander, the best cross-examiner in Britain, possibly in the world…'

'Okay,' said Kerry, 'We'll have him.'

The guy coughed and went on, 'Then there's Mr Andrew Merritt who's easily the best in the country on this particular point of law…'

'Great,' said Kerry, 'we'll have him too.'

'They were gobsmacked,' says Greig, "Mr Packer, you're not serious. You can't have *two* QCs".'

Yes he could. Kerry ended up retaining both QCs, plus their legal teams. For the next two months Mr Justice Slade's courtroom had more legal brains sitting round on its benches than it had room in the public gallery.

Summers of cricket, in both hemispheres, have developed idiosyncratic sporting moments that have made their way into the touring culture. One of these is the haphazardly organised one-day match between the press of the home side and the touring journalists. All sorts of fringe characters end up playing in this game, but the cricket is of a fairly high standard – many of the cricketing press are pretty handy on a cricket field. In 1977 this match was held on 14 August, the rest day of the Fourth Test, at the county oval Harrogate in northern Yorkshire.

The day before the game Ian Chappell was visiting Kerry in his Dorchester suite when a call came through for him. On the other end was *Age* journalist Peter McFarline, one of the Australian journalists who'd busted the original WSC story prematurely wide open and the author of an article on Kerry that noted he not only looked like a hammerhead shark, but acted like one. McFarline, captain of the Australian Press XI, had earlier recruited Chappell into his team but was having trouble making up his numbers. Chappell, Mr Mischievous, put his hand over the phone, turned to Kerry and asked him if he'd like a game of cricket on Sunday – for the Australian media. 'I think you qualify,' he said. Kerry agreed to play. Caught, Chappell added, 'Peter McFarline's the captain of the team, will that cause a problem?' According to Chappell, Kerry thought for a moment, then said 'No, that's not a problem'.

At Harrogate the next day Kerry found himself not only playing alongside McFarline, but the other breaker of his story, Alan Shiell, and lo and behold, his most bitter critic and Jeff Thomson's agent, David Lord. It's not recorded whether the two snarled at each other as they walked onto the field. The Australians batted first. Kerry came in to bat at number eight, faced seven balls and scored a nifty two not out. During the English team's innings Alan Shiell tired of keeping wicket, looked around to see if anyone else wanted a go with the gloves. Kerry, who had been a part-time wicketkeeper at school, stepped in.

'So Kerry's keeping,' says Ian Chappell, 'and who's bowling but Lordy.' David Lord had played handy club cricket for Mosman in Sydney. He ran in with a medium pace ball to the batsman, Peter Lush, press officer for Kerry's other sworn enemy, the TCCB. Lush nicked it. Kerry swooped and Lush was caught behind. Somewhere in the depths of some cricket vault is a scoreline: Lush, caught Packer, bowled Lord.

In the sunshine, amidst laughter and cheers from the Australian media and a few scattered boos and catcalls from the English spectators, Chappell at first slip then witnessed David Lord dashing down the pitch to congratulate a grinning Kerry, the two enemies patting each other on the back.

'All this hugging and stuff they go on with now, that's more of a recent thing,' says Chappell. 'But there was backslapping and congratulations. Lordy's come up and he's slapping Kerry saying well done.' The Australians won the match and later Kerry joined Lord, Lush, McFarline and the rest of his critics in the dressing room, happily chatting about the game and cricket in general. 'Which just goes to show,' said Chappell, 'how much sport can help solve a lot of problems'.

It didn't solve anything of course, but it probably put Kerry into a more humane light for many of the journalists. As Henry Blofeld put it, 'Only cricket could have produced such an absurd situation'.

The cricket drama now developed and expanded into its cutthroat, and inevitable, legal phase. In the words of Chris Forsyth, 'The enemy had WSC encircled and was tightening the ring. The Establishment's cricket commanders seemed far-sighted in their strategy; and WSC could see only what was under its nose. The cricket revolution was halted mid-stride by legal entanglements in Sydney and London'.

In the final week of September, Bob Parish and Ray Steele noticed a four-page insert in Kerry's *The Australian Women's Weekly* singing the praises of WSC, using the words 'Australia', 'The World' and 'The West Indies' with a whole lot of coloured pics of Ian Chappell, Rod Marsh, Dennis Lillee, Alan Knott and Clive Lloyd in the traditional colours of their countries. And worse,

Chappell and Marsh were wearing the sacred 'baggy green' caps of Australia. Parish and Steele sniffed an opportunity to at least land some sort of body blow. They applied for an injunction in the Federal Court to stop WSC using the words 'Test' or 'Test Series' to describe WSC games, or the words 'Australia' or 'the Australian Team' to describe the players.

It was a nicely timed move. The whole WSC caravan had its mind on the upcoming High Court case in London with Greig, Procter and Snow and their lawyers and barristers huddled together, cramming for what would no doubt be a harrowing experience. Kerry was in London overseeing the whole thing.

'It was an ambush,' wrote Forsyth, 'and like all well-mounted ambushes it caught the entire WSC operation on the wrong foot'. The kicker was that in its glossy four-page promo WSC had stated that 'All matches played in the Supertest, International Cup and Country Cup series will be conducted and played under accepted international cricket laws and standards'. Words like this, said the ACB, were likely to mislead the punters into thinking that WSC had the imprimatur of the authorities. Kerry's QC Murray Gleeson got stuck right into that one. After the highly visible hostilities, the poaching of 51 of the world's best cricketers, the screaming headlines, the TV interviews, total turmoil in the cricketing world and the pitch for the hearts and minds of the cricketing public from the ICC, the TCCB and the ACB, could any Australian, anywhere, he said, be misled into thinking the ACB had actually given Super-tests the official tick?

In the Sydney court a few days later, Justice St John decided that just such badly informed people might exist, and they'd probably be reading the *The Australian Women's Weekly*. He decided the *Weekly* insert, on the whole, could be misleading and was not to be used again. He took a look at six upcoming TV ads for WSC, put together by John Cornell, which used the same terms as the printed version and decided two had to be scrapped altogether and slapped a restraining order on another. Finally he granted an interim injunction stopping WSC from any further use of the word 'Australia' to describe the rebel Aussie players or referring to them as 'the Australian team'. Bob Parish declared himself pleased. Kerry declared he would appeal.

It got worse. After the NSW Government sacked the SCG Trust and replaced it with a new board, WSC had been given permission to use the SCG for a period of 17 days over the coming December and January. But the NSW Cricket Association suddenly decided to challenge that in the Equity Court, arguing that the WSC dates would clash with Grade cricket matches. WSC still had the Sydney Showground up its sleeve, but this was yet another indicator that the authorities were fighting over every inch of ground.

★

The main legal game now opened in England's High Court in London before Mr Justice Slade, both sides sitting about the ancient court on hard timber benches, two of the most uncomfortable being the long and lanky Tony Greig and the massively framed Kerry beside him, nicking out at various intervals to light up yet another cigarette. The case started on 26 September 1977 when Alexander QC got up and spoke for two days. It then rolled on for the next seven weeks with witness after witness being called, examined and cross-examined. Alexander, a towering and overwhelming figure in court, called nine witnesses and his opponent Michael Kempster QC called twelve.

Here again was an example of the cultural and generational divide between WSC and its opponents. The Establishment figures, all conformist ageing men, arrived in court in conservatively-cut suits and Windsor-knotted ties, short-haired and pressed, then underlined their image with headmasterly tones and a haughty demeanour in the witness box. By contrast, the WSC mob were from Mars, or the future. 'The Packer contingent seemed to represent a totally different lifestyle,' wrote Henry Blofeld. 'Richie Benaud wore light-coloured suits, crocodile shoes and flashing ties. Another supporter was dressed in a splurge of yellow, while from another there was a flash of orange leather. John Snow's unruly hair usually flopped out of a roll-necked sweater.'

During the whole scrap Tony Greig in the witness box was particularly savaged by Kempster, later describing it as 'a gruelling exercise'. Greig, copping it yet again, must have wondered when all this was going to end. For day after day Greig, Procter, Snow, Ross Edwards, Alan Knott and Derek Underwood put their positions, hating the long hours of unfamiliar pressure of cross-examination. These were men who thrived on competition and confrontation – but not like this. Still, they held up and their theme was consistent – before Kerry came into their lives to give them certainty and respect they were universally underpaid and badly treated and every one of them was concerned about the lack of any long-term prospects to financially protect their families.

The ICC's 12 witnesses included the ACB's Ray Steele, ICC Secretary Jack Bailey, Doug Insole, and a speaker each from the West Indies board, the New Zealand Cricket Council and the Indian and Pakistani boards, every one with tales to tell of the terrible damage WSC was doing to the cricket world. Commentators have pointed out that Sir Donald Bradman, who probably had more clout than any of these others, chose to stay well clear. Gideon Haigh quotes Ray Steele on the great man's absence, 'He was such a shrewd little bugger, of course'. The official excuse was reported to be that Bradman's wife was ill at the time. Steele stepped up for Bradman, insisting that the proposed ban on the players was in his view 'eminently reasonable'. Doug Insole put it plainest – the authorities, he said, were 'totally concerned with what was lawful and, at the same time, totally concerned with the best interests of English cricket'. The ICC's actions had been simply to 'protect' their game.

All these middle-aged men, honestly believing in the rightness of their cause and clearly articulating it, made solid arguments for the defensive position they'd taken as soon as Kerry had appeared over the rise. They led with their hearts, their eyes filled with the glow of a century of cricket purity, stating honestly and with conviction their deep belief in a cricket world of certain certainties. But even as they spoke so forthrightly from the witness box, commentators and legal experts in London and Sydney doubted just how well their words went to convincing *anyone,* let alone the judge, that their ban on the cricketers was not in restraint of trade.

As well as his brace of autumnal administrators, Kempster called up two tough-guy Yorkshireman cricketers. Into the witness box came Ray Illingworth, a shrewd and rock-solid former England captain with a reputation as a brilliant tactician, one of the few English captains taken to the hearts of the Australian cricketing public. Even as Illingworth's team stopped Australia in the Ashes Series of 1970–71 and again in 1972 the Aussie ocker punter remained respectful, even fond of, this hard man. From the witness box in his characteristic blunt way Illingworth said if he had still been playing cricket and had been offered a WSC contract, he would have 'considered it very carefully'. But he went on to say if he had signed up he would have expected to be excluded from Establishment cricket.

The other Yorkshireman was the legendary Geoffrey Boycott, prickly, controversial, a massively talented batsman who polarised the cricketing public around the world. Either you loved Boycott or you hated him – the same people appearing on opposite sides of the debate at different periods in his life. He was charged at various times with ducking the best fast bowlers of his era by making himself unavailable for certain games and by an at times glacial consolidation of runs – that very year he spent ten and a half hours at the crease for 191. It was also claimed that he often concentrated on his own batting statistics to the detriment of his team's overall performance – yet statistics show that of his 108 tests for England (during which he scored more than 8000 runs), the team only lost 20 when Boycott was playing and if he scored a century England always won that match.

Boycott told the court how he had been offered a contract by Kerry, but after getting into a snarl about whether he would captain the World Team, the two had moved apart. He was consistently orthodox in his anti-WSC views, pulling out the apt homily that a man cannot serve two masters – the same point as Illingworth – that WSC players shouldn't be allowed to pocket large sums from Kerry and still expect to play their usual English County and International matches. 'They can't,' as he folksily put it, 'have the penny and the bun'.

Lynton Taylor and Kerry were the two senior WSC operatives called to the witness box. Examined by Alexander Kerry played it straight, telling the court he was already committed to putting $12 million into WSC in the next few years. During questioning by Alexander about his reasons for moving into the cricket world he replied lightly, 'Contrary to public opinion I have always liked cricket. I have always been a little resentful of the fact that I was never coached properly'. He and Alexander question by question, answer by answer, painted a slick picture of well-intentioned innovation in the game coming up against an unfortunate brick wall of crusty old farts who had their own well-being at heart (in court Kerry described the ACB leaders as 'grossly incompetent'). WSC would bring huge benefits to the players and the public and to TV and it was an all-round good thing for cricket itself, bringing fresh life and energy to the great game.

Finally Alexander took his seat and it was time for Kerry to be cross-examined by Kempster. This was the moment everyone on the hard timber seats had been waiting for. Kempster had a reputation as a rapier-sharp and crafty cross-examiner and Kerry was a man who could explode, lose it completely, if pressed too hard. And to make things worse he was about to go through an ordeal of many hours without a cigarette. The WSC operatives and a few of the journalists knew what kind of Packer surfaced if Kerry was deprived of nicotine for even a short period of time, and Kempster was clearly going to do his best to get under his skin. Kempster's tactic was to try to lay bare the superficial opportunism of a businessman who wasn't in this for cricket or the cricketers but simply to add to his millions.

In the court were John Cornell and Paul Hogan, sitting with fingers crossed. As Kerry stepped into the witness box, Cornell turned to Hogan, 'I said to Hoges this'll either be a total disaster or a triumph'.

It didn't take Kempster long to hit Kerry with the big one. 'Is it right,' he asked, 'that you went into the Supertest business to make money?'

'Of course.' Kerry replied calmly, 'I've never said anything else'.

Silence. Up the back there were a few quiet chuckles. Kempster adjusted his wig and plunged on. It came out later that the eminent QC adjusted his wig on his head if he was struggling with a difficult witness. He bowled up his next question. Kerry whacked it back and the game proceeded.

'I'll never forget it,' said Cornell, 'Kerry was so good that the QC ended up twisting his wig on his head out of frustration so much it ended up with the plait *in front* of his ear instead of behind it'. For a day and a half Kempster thrust and probed, and for a day and a half Kerry managed to play Mr Intelligent. In the BBC studio with David Frost and Robin Marlar he had been the unexpectedly ironic smiling man with warmth and charm to burn. A man of the people. In the Dorchester suite facing his reluctant players he was the dominant alpha mensch who could lead you to the promised land. Now here he was in this ancient academic context calmly sparring with one of the foremost legal intellects of his day. And winning.

'He was absolutely brilliant,' says Cornell, 'That was

the first time I'd ever seen him be that good. I knew then that he was going to make this huge mark. We saw him arriving'.

Kerry would not have performed in quite such an impressive way five years earlier. His first hesitant foray into a business that was his alone, independent of dominance by his father, was the women's magazine *Cleo* with editor Ita Buttrose. It was only in 1974, with *Cleo* a smash and old Sir Frank dead, that Kerry, dyslexic and uncertain, began to shake off at last his father's 'boofhead' tag. Rid of the man who had brutalised him and buoyed by the money pouring in from the overwhelming success of his own magazine, Kerry went into WSC with freshly acquired confidence – and he came out three years later with a clear understanding of power and how to use it. The days of his cricket war were the days when Kerry stepped out from beneath the old man's shadow, forging an independent view of the world and of himself. Throughout the saga the cricket authorities were dealing with a mercurial figure who was in the process of inventing the Kerry Packer of legend. He was a moving target and history shows they never quite understood him. From the moment of the death of his father, the Consolidated Press profit graph began to tilt – who would have believed it – northwards, and through the cricket imbroglio and beyond, it kept improving. (In 1977, only his third year at the helm, the company profit was more than 50 per cent up on the previous year.) By the time WSC was behind him Kerry was a formidable and courageous entrepreneur, a confident operator, an enterprising buccaneer who could mix it with the big guns of international business. He took over from his father a local publishing enterprise worth at best a few tens of millions and when he died in 2005 he left a global empire reported at various amounts but always within whispering distance of $6.5 billion dollars.

Getting a sense of his burgeoning power during the court case, Kerry completely dominated his two highly sophisticated QCs and their legal teams. He declared that because he was paying them good money he didn't want them sneaking off at any point during the case and working on other briefs, so they all had to join him at lunch each day and again after the court rose. He hired the top floor of the ancient Wig and Pen Club, just across the street from the courts. The Wig and Pen – where journalists and barristers would meet during court cases (hence the name) was in an ancient gatekeepers' home, a building that survived the Great Fire of London in 1666, reputed to be haunted by the headless ghost of Oliver Cromwell. The stained glass at its front has the words: 'Go thy way, eat thy bread with joy and drink thy wine with a merry heart, for God approveth thy work'.

Watching his brilliant QCs at work and approving highly, Kerry began enjoying himself. Each day at luncheon in the Wig and Pen he'd have what he termed a 'team talk' discussing the case and its developments. After he had been beating Geoffrey Boycott up in the witness box all one morning, Alexander told Kerry at lunch that he'd finished his cross-examination of the opposition champion batsman. 'No,' said Kerry, 'Get him back this afternoon and get stuck into him for another few hours'. Alexander did.

Kerry held a QC competition, eagerly followed by the legal team and the cricketers and WSC insiders who turned up for lunch. He pinned a large map of the world on the timber wall panels of the Wig and Pen room. 'You win this case,' he told Alexander and Merritt, pointing to the map, 'and you and your families are coming with me for the best holiday you've had in your life. Right down here in Australia. At lunch each day we're going to plot your course and see how you go'.

He stuck coloured pin markers into the map, beginning in London. From then on, if Kerry considered the barristers had a successful day, the markers would be moved towards Australia – Paris, Rome, Athens, Dubai … the Aussie holiday getting closer daily. If Kerry was unhappy the pins would be set back a stage or so. One lunchtime he decided they'd not been functioning very well at all so he sent them both all the way back to London to start again.

The case continued for 31 full days. When the final submission was made and silence fell in court Mr Justice Slade told the assembled press and team members from both sides that he would write up his decision as quickly as possible but, 'I have a certain amount of work to do'.

That day the Wig and Pen get-together after the case closed – drinks and a lavish afternoon tea – was like the dressing room after a good game, the mood buoyant, positive. Cornell says he approached Kerry and told him he'd just witnessed his finest innings. 'Mate', he said, 'you just got 196 not out'. He noticed Kerry wasn't listening, but standing there with a piggish look on his face. Cornell looked across and saw Lynton Taylor hovering over the splendid afternoon feast. At the close of the whole drama, 'Kerry just wanted to finish talking and get to the cakes himself before Lynton ate them all'.

★

Meanwhile outside the court the cricket battle was still raging. During the period of the High Court case local authorities all over the world were very busy indeed fulfilling the agreement they made with the ICC. Not waiting for Mr Justice Slade to hand down his judgment they plunged on with disciplinary action against their cricketers. Despite reported ructions within the board itself, the WICBC announced it would go along with the ICC ban and exclude all its WSC cricketers from the official West Indies XI. The West Indies cricketers hit back immediately, questioning the WICBC's legal right to exclude them and insisting that all the WSC West Indies players would be available if needed for Test cricket. It did them no good.

In New Zealand, the New Zealand Cricket Council (NCC) followed up by banning any cricketer from playing for New Zealand if they signed up with anyone else. The Board of Control for Cricket in Pakistan (BCCP) banned five of its stars from playing cricket anywhere in the world. All five were WSC signatories.

In Australia, the ACB, more intimately involved, chose to play it differently. In a fine Catch-22 move it was announced that because the High Court case was still pending there would be no blanket ban on WSC players. Instead they would be invited to sign a contract to play for Australia and paid more, a minimum of $1852 per official Test (money from a new sponsorship deal with the Benson & Hedges cigarettes). But the players were already signed to Kerry so they couldn't now sign up to play traditional cricket. They'd excluded themselves. QED.

Beneath the ACB in the Australian hierarchy of the game, there were plenty of minor administrators who were on a war footing and not in any mood to be so clever or subtle. The rot crept down into state level, then further down into district cricket. Max Walker, Richie Robinson and Ray Bright were sacked from the Victorian State practice squad. In New South Wales, Doug Walters, Rick McCosker, Len Pascoe, Kerry O'Keefe, Gary Gilmour and Ian Davis copped the same treatment. In Perth, the West Australian Cricket Association (WACA) banned not only Rod Marsh, Mick Malone, Ross Edwards and Bruce Laird, but the favourite son, Dennis Lillee, from playing at state or club level. (Lillee ignored the ban and kept training with and coaching his local Melville club. For this not-to-be-countenanced breach the WACA banned Lillee from using the club facilities, then, finding it could only fine Melville $5, did so, threatening to change the rules in the future.)

Max Walker was dumped as captain of Melbourne. Ian Chappell and Ian Redpath, highly respected senior players who had retired from Test and state cricket but had kept their eye in by playing the District game (Chappell for North Melbourne and Redpath for South Melbourne) were also excluded. In his case, Chappell had already voluntarily withdrawn from North Melbourne but decided he might play for his local Adelaide team Glenelg. No way. Glenelg officials were told by the ACB that all funding to the club would be withdrawn if Chappell so much as picked up a bat.

Redpath in particular, who had spent 20 years with South Melbourne and was a life member and celebrated fixture of the place, was reported to have been particularly hurt. Being banned at the international level along with the rest of the global elite was part of the grand strategic game being played out and easier to swallow than pariah status at home amongst your close long-term friends and team-mates. The guys who had played their instruments in the grandest concert theatres in the world were now reduced to busking on street corners. In a game way beneath the authorities' radar, Max Walker fronted up to play for the Old Scotch Collegians in Melbourne. Gideon Haigh quotes Walker, 'I'd gone from crowds of sixty-five, seventy thousand in the Centenary Test, to two blokes, one lady and a dog'.

★

As the court cases played themselves out and the world's sporting press kept up either it's loud condemnation or its happy approval of WSC, as the executives worked through until the early hours of the morning, as the players laughed or fretted or just sat around waiting for something to happen, Kerry was spending money. He had been spending a truckload since that day, which already seemed so far off, when John Cornell first came to him with an idea. And in the days to come he would be spending a whole lot more.

We all know the 'Hero's Journey', beloved of story-tellers, screenwriters and songwriters, the thousands-of-years-old paradigmatic story structure where a 'hero' is called to go out into an unknown world on a quest. The paradigm can have a lot of filigree and layers, but essentially this guy (by tradition a male) steps into the unknown, is faced with impossibly difficult tasks, goes through one particularly hellish time when he is swallowed into the unknown – known as 'the belly of the whale' – before finally winning and returning home, having changed the world for the better. On this journey, sometimes accompanied by those who believe in him, the hero is advised by a gnomic figure who imparts wisdom and truth, and he learns about himself and the world from this mysterious person from the shadows. Through the time of WSC Kerry had just such a figure – an Obi-Wan Kenobi character in the form of the high priest of CPH – Harry Chester.

Described by Henry Blofeld as 'the most influential figure in Packer's realm', Chester was deputy chairman of CPH and had been since the death in 1974 of old Sir Frank Packer. When Sir Frank went he left Chester as a trustee of his will and in charge of young Kerry (who Chester called 'Kerro'), and through the whole of Kerry's journey this was the only man who could nail him down and lecture him on where the hell he was going wrong. By all accounts he was a genial grey-haired fellow, brilliant with a balance sheet, charming to women and from his first day at CPH in the late sixties, a benign force in the corridors. One senior CPH executive described him as 'the Rock of Gibraltar type … a terrific guy, terribly honest, very straight up and down and uncomplicated'.

Kerry adored Chester and heard his wisdom, partly because in the early days Chester had the personal strength and enough influence with Sir Frank to protect Kerry from some of the old man's bullying excesses. Not only that, Chester nurtured Kerry and encouraged him, taking the traditional fond uncle role, a soul-inspiring change from the aggressive humiliation dished out by the father. In October 1979 Chester, only 58, died of a heart attack sitting in a chair out the back of his home on Sydney's North Shore. There is no report of how dry-eyed or not he was at the death of his father, but when he heard of Chester's sudden death, Kerry, at the family farm 'Ellerston' near Scone in New South Wales, went for a walk on the property and wept.

Chester, genial man, was also pragmatic, resourceful and plain tough, with a killer's instinct and a hard-as-nails attitude to getting the job done. Known as 'Harry the Hatchet', he threw fear into CPH operatives and used his immense power in the organisation with ruthless efficiency. As financial controller he kept an eye on every cent Kerry and his gang of WSC fellow-travellers spent, and through 1977 he believed they were tossing it around quite a bit, carpeting Kerry at irregular intervals to remind the young tyro that the company Chester was running was ultimately funding all this cricket nonsense.

Kerry was a businessman who didn't mind tossing cash at a problem, but at least he was throwing his own money. Kerry's free-handed ways during WSC drifted down to his operatives and gave Chester heart palpitations. In London, the Dorchester was the abode of choice for the senior WSC executives who popped in and out of their elegant £1000-a-night suites, racking up all sorts of expenses in the name of the cricket revolution and Chester, all-seeing, observed every move they made. Chris Forsyth, working as hard as anyone as chief publicity guy, said any memo from Chester equated with 'a knock on the door from the NKVD in Stalin's Soviet Union'. Obviously aware of the executives' footloose handling of money, Chester whipped one such memo to General Manager Vern Stone, declaring control over the money 'not good enough'. 'I want you to give me details of any expenditure incurred without your prior approval and in particular who was responsible,' he snarled, 'I will make it my business to prevent any recurrence'.

Chester kept shoving his finger in the dyke but knew he was struggling to stop leaks all over the place. 'Wastage through inefficiency, anxiety, indecision and bad management pushed the bill up,' says Forsyth, 'The wastage was widespread and came from profligate use of the advertising budget, misunderstandings, delays and duplications'.

By late spring of 1977, the outlay was astonishing. Kerry had rolled out nearly $1.5 million to his players, who were also on $115 a week expenses. He'd kicked in $775,000 on ground hire (VFL Park alone cost $825,000 over three years, the SCG $200,000 for 17 days), and another $425,000 on getting Maley's pitches right. TV coverage of the games was already $1.4 million. The coaching program, using the cricket stars to help up and coming cricketers, was a $200,000 outlay. Then there was travel, accommodation (95 suites at the Old Melbourne were booked for players families and administrators), airfares, legal expenses, executives' salaries, umpires fees, advertising, players' prizemoney, clothing and equipment, curators, masseurs, various other overheads – and the list went on. Harry Chester had estimated the cost of the first year at about $4.5 million, but it no doubt kicked well above that.

Who knows how much Kerry was willing to toss into this maw, how much of the company's money he had secretly decided he was willing to lose on this pet project, independent of any official financial understandings with his mentor Chester. But while figures of five and six million were being tossed around, on 28 October, Forsyth says Kerry snapped at him, 'Get the legal side straight. If you fuck up, we could lose the whole thing – we could lose the whole twelve million'. 'Clearly the remark of an extremely nervous man,' he added.

To claw back something at this dark time when the whole caravan was still stalled in various courts, Kerry was hammering his executives to get out there and sell, sell, sell. He threw lavish dinners in Melbourne and Sydney for prospective sponsors, wining and dining them in sumptuous style, showing them specially shot promos featuring some of his star players, all pushing the idea that there'd be wonderful benefits for anyone smart enough to get into this on the ground floor. In a major blitz they went all out, swamping major sponsors and corporations with an innovative sales pitch of TV and magazine ads, ground perimeter advertising boards and spots in the officially printed programs and, a first for cricket, insisting that women consumers would be there at the games. Eric Beecher in his 1978 book on WSC, *The Cricket Revolution,* noted, 'For the first time in its history cricket was presented as a modern, well-researched medium for selling products to mass audiences'.

The sales team had some success, but not enough for Kerry who hit the road himself, pulling out all his super-salesman techniques, charming, bullying and cajoling his marks, who mostly kept their hands in their pockets. Advertisers are traditionally wary of the new, as Kerry and Ita Buttrose had discovered when they first started trying to sell advertising in the fresh and untried *Cleo.* Ad agency execs prefer to wait for success and are then quite happy to pay the premium.

Kerry might have been nervous – must have been nervous – and we know he wasn't sleeping at night, but he blustered and bluffed, forging on, keeping any thoughts of disaster to himself. His publicity operatives had kept up pugnacious rhetoric about how WSC was on the edge of making big profits. But in November when he spoke to *The Australian* journalist Philip Cornford, Kerry, for some reason decided to come clean. In what Cornford later described as 'a devastating contradiction of what his publicity machine had been hammering down the throats of the media – that World Series would make a profit', Kerry had said the first season of

WSC would cost $6 million while gate receipts at the grounds, sponsorship and TV revenue would bring in only about $4 million.

'So we take a loss of $2 million,' Kerry told Cornford, 'so what? I couldn't buy all that top television time, 315 hours of it, for one million dollars, so that cuts the loss to a million. After tax it's $500,000. Am I going to suffer fits of apoplexia at night worrying about half a million dollars?'

The revelation broke in *The Australian* the following day. When publicity boss Chris Forsyth arrived in the press box for a WSC match a short time later, a journalist who had copped it from his office for missing the story, attacked him with a rolled-up copy of his newspaper.

★

The Australian summer arrived with its blazing hot Brisbane and Melbourne days. Sydney is said to have three elements that characterise summer – afternoon thunderstorms, cicadas and cricket. In freezing London, Mr Justice Slade was in his cosy chambers working on his judgment that, either way, was going to have a massive impact on WSC and the game in general. But it was no good trying to second-guess His Honour or make any decisions based on what he may or may not come up with. It was time for Kerry and his band to fish or cut bait. They'd been cutting bait for many months and the non-negotiable moment of truth had finally arrived.

WSC cricket was in the headlines and in the courts and in press statements and administrative memos, it was in people's minds and in their imaginations, it was everywhere except on the fields. With the first all-important matches looming and the Test cricketers back in Australia from their drubbing in England it was time for the players to bond over training.

The Pakistanis, the South Africans, the West Indians and the English players landed Downunder, many for the first time with wives and children – another WSC revolution – to begin the great adventure. First there was official training at St Kilda Football Club where the players began at last doing what they did best. It was a relief, after the diplomacy and the doubt, after all those press conferences and dreadful newspaper headlines, all the hissing and insults from true believers amongst the public, to at last get a bat or a ball in their hands. To get the gloves on. Here they were in summer sunshine on green grass, at the crease, using their bodies. They were the finest cricketers in the world and they knew it – some of the finest who had ever played the game. Now they could show the people out there why they had signed up – not for the money, but to do this, to make remarkable and unforgettable things happen on a sporting field. They threw themselves into training.

Most eager amongst them were the South Africans Eddie Barlow, Mike Procter and Barry Richards who had spent the last seven summers playing England's County cricket, reduced to watching their international peers on the TV, knowing they were easily able to mix it with the best but unable to because of politics. As key elements of the WSC World side they were itching to get a crack at top-class opposition and hanging out for a chance to have their skills tested against the best players. But now, like Mohammad Ali, their key years of talent had been denied them and deep down they must have each worried whether they could cut the mustard with the very best, and how many good years they might have left.

Kerry always insisted that his troops train their hearts out. He was, after all, paying them good money and he didn't want them thinking this was going to be any sort of cakewalk. There were fines for skipping training or slacking off and Kerry would arrive at unexpected times at the nets or on the training fields to check on how things were developing. The players trained for eight-hour days – warm-up exercises followed by sprints and longer runs, stretching and strengthening exercises, catching practice, bowling and batting in the nets, the young guns training with their boyhood heroes. Training. This is what elite sportsmen and women have always done and must always do. It's the absolute essence of their profession. But this time there was an added pressure – they were stepping into the unknown.

The critical first moment came at 11 o'clock in the morning of Thursday, 24 November 1977 in blazing sunshine at Melbourne's VFL Park. A three-day game between the Australians led by Ian Chappell and the World led by Tony Greig. Headlines all over the sports press reminded everyone that at last WSC had arrived at its judgment day. Here was the acid test. John Maley's pitch had been laid in the centre of the vast football arena, the outfield had been mowed and rolled, the stumps were propped and bail-ready. Inside the huge stadium press box phones were set up for reporters, stalls were set up selling WSC badges, T-shirts and hats, and up in the VIP area a fine spread was laid on for insiders.

The day started in a hollow silence – and got worse. As Kerry and John Cornell checked through binoculars from high in the concrete structure, outside the 10-hectare carpark was all but empty, just a scattering of cars – one here and there. According to Chris Forsyth, 'a 40-seater bus drew up and set down three passengers'. WSC insiders had been punting amongst themselves on the size of this first crowd. Would it be 5000, 8000,

10,000 – maybe as many as 20,000? Not much in an arena that holds nearly 80,000. But at a few minutes to 11 the cavernous place held just over 200 people. When the cricketers walked out onto the field into the sunshine what they saw was a deserted stadium, and what they heard was hollow, desultory clapping from a handful of spectators. Tony Greig looked around horrified. 'I was quite sure there were more people in the VIP area than in the stands,' he wrote later.

Up in the gods, Kerry was looking down on the worst possible scenario for his hopes and dreams and for his stubborn insistence that he could make all this work. He knew the English High Court decision was to be delivered in a day or so, and if that went against him he would have to make a whole new beginning. Truly he had arrived in the belly of the whale.

3
COMPLICATION

Mr Justice Slade stepped into his court on the morning of Friday, 25 November 1977 and proceeded to deliver his judgment. It was 211 pages long, it took him 5 ½ hours to read. When he finally put his papers down, WSC existed in a different universe. His Honour had found comprehensively in favour of Tony Greig, Mike Procter and John Snow. He examined in detail nine legal points – putting to himself nine legal questions – and he answered them all, one at a time, in favour of WSC. The Establishment didn't take a trick. And to add to the pain, costs were awarded against the ICC and the TCCB – they were hit with a legal bill of more than $320,000.

Sure enough, the cricket bans on the players were in restraint of trade and the authorities had acted against the law in trying to stop the players earning a living from their cricketing abilities. The judge said he understood and even to a certain extent sympathised with the authorities point of view in all this, they were clearly doing what they thought was in the best interests of cricket and they had an 'understandable desire to make things as difficult as possible for Mr Packer'. But he found the official bodies guilty of pressurising the cricketers to break their contracts with WSC and legally wrong in banning the players. The bans were, he declared, null and void.

He went further than anyone expected, saying everything short of 'gimme a break', pointing out that, given the authorities' vengeful reaction when they first heard about WSC, he couldn't *blame* the cricketers for keeping their signings a secret. He decided it was about bloody time the players were paid what they were worth and pointed out that the TCCB had made $1.6 million from the players last year. If the players had been paid decent money this whole thing might not have happened, and because the players were getting screwed this sort of challenge to traditional cricket 'was bound to come sooner rather than later'. He even found WSC to be a good thing for cricket. The Packer organisation had aided the game by offering good money for a good days' work, by bringing fresh sponsors to the game, by initiating the kids' coaching scheme and by bringing cricket back to the public in a refreshing new way.

Kerry's barristers had earned their all-expenses family holidays in Australia. Kerry couldn't have got a better judgment if he'd written it himself. He sat up nervously alone in his suite in Melbourne's Hotel Australia and got the news in the early hours of the morning, immediately ringing Tony Greig, fast asleep down at the Old Melbourne, and telling him of the triumph. The next morning Mr Happy went down to the Old Melbourne and had breakfast with John Cornell, tucking into a huge plate of food, smiling around at his tribe who had all heard the good news. The sun might not have come out, but it was at last peeking from behind the clouds. Chris Forsyth quotes Kerry, 'That'll serve 'em right. Maybe they won't be so ready to tangle with me again – not if it costs them that kind of money every time'.

Asked if it was maybe time to come to some sort of compromise with the authorities he was blunt, triumphant. 'They'll have to come to me,' he said, 'I've done all the compromising up to now, I'm going to leave it to them to make the first move'.

Having been granted it on a plate by Sir Christopher, Kerry took every advantage and bolted up the high ground. 'Maybe I'm not the villain I was painted to be,' he said, 'My faith in British justice is restored.' He elevated his rhetoric, telling the press that the decision was 'all about human rights' and how human rights had just taken a giant step forward. Asked if he expected the ACB to now come to him he replied, 'It would be easier to get an audience with the Pope. And I'm not a Catholic'.

The bombshell hit the ACB, the TCCB and the ICC hard. They withdrew to their bunkers, no doubt with the same lawyers who had given them the costly legal advice in the first place, and tried to decide their next move. The loss would have done their attitude no good at all. Kerry's new challenge to them to come to him, was, as they saw it, nothing more than a bit of cheap Aussie crowing. In Melbourne sports journalists chased down Bob Parish and Ray Steele of the ACB, but they had gone to ground, issuing an official and sniffy no comment. In London the TCCB chairman Doug Insole showed a little more grace, declaring, 'We were well and truly stuffed'.

The old men of the boards must have wondered what they had done to deserve such a terrible beating. They had reacted as gentlemen, to be sure, morally indignant at what had been done to their game and doing their best to play by cricket's fine and traditional conventions of fair play and honour. But suddenly that wasn't enough. The barbarians had arrived at their gates with all their nasty new ways, all their rejection of history and disrespect for the past, and the gates had been happily swung open by that most ancient and hallowed institution, the English court system. It wasn't fair. They had the whole time acted in a way they thought was right and proper. A perfect example of this was their agreement to disclose the informal shorthand notes of their meetings on the WSC matter, which did them a lot of damage in court. By contrast, when Kerry was asked for the similar notes of his meetings it was found that, most unfortunately, someone had shredded them.

The authorities now realised their enemy was the future of cricket – the game they loved and fought for had just lost something of its essence. The case underlined the size of the chasm between the two sides, the basic contradiction between them. In their own way the Establishment had put the game first. It was time-honoured custom, unquestioned for a century, that they were the representative and responsible bodies, the keepers of the keys, and they honoured that commitment on behalf of the players. But the players saw themselves as the soul of the game. Cricket would not exist without them – the boards were administrators and booking agents, nothing more. And they hadn't been doing much of a job for the players on the front line for quite a while.

Mr Justice Slade's historic decision came down on day two of that first three-day match at VFL Park. After the disastrous start, when two men and a dog had turned up to see the first ball bowled, things had improved some-what and, at its peak, that first WSC day had a crowd of nearly 2500 – better, but still looking like nothing more than a sprinkling in the huge arena. Photos in the press showed mainly empty sun-drenched concrete bleach-ers with a single spectator sitting here and there. WSC insiders complained later that these shots had been set up by the photographers: 'Excuse me sir, can you come over here and sit by yourself?'

It didn't matter much because Kerry and the others had moved the goalposts. Like kids playing marbles in the schoolyard where the first go, if it misses, is always deemed a 'practice shot', the game – which initially had been part of the official schedule – had merely been a 'trial match', they said. Nothing official, the crowd didn't count, we were testing our equipment, putting our big toe in the water, just kicking the tyres. You just wait until a real game.

Even so, as a trial it went reasonably well. Another few hundred spectators turned up for day two and by day three there were 3500 people in the stands. Ian Chappell scored the first WSC century (118 not out) and John Maley's freshly grown wicket not only held up well but was considered by the players to be as good as anything they'd played on.

Press reaction was a mixed bag and would have given

the WSC not much comfort. In *The Age*, Peter McFarline said WSC had started 'with the explosion of a mid week fixture between the Plastic XI and Bill's Bookshop'. But the other Australian reporters just yawned a bit, took note of the score and listed what they liked and didn't like about the game – not overly enthusiastic or particularly scathing. They were holding fire till the real games, the Supertests, came along. By contrast, their English brethren agreed with McFarline and gave the game quite a bit of stick, their theme being that somehow, and not unexpectedly, WSC had drained the noble game of its excitement and intrigue. Who cares if the players are making a quid? They're playing for themselves, not for their countries. And it shows.

Henry Blofeld was up in the stands. 'I watched from the press box, and after two hours realised I had been talking continuously to friends and had seen less than half the balls bowled. I had made an effort to concentrate and had found it difficult,' he wrote, 'It seemed extraordinary that less than a thousand people should have been in the ground at the start, but gradually one began to realise that those who stayed away might have been good judges after all ... One was acutely conscious of how dead the game seemed. If the result does not matter the means of achieving it does not matter either.'

He witnessed an appeal by the World players against

Greg Chappell, given not out by the umpire. The players involved then 'grinned at each other'. According to Blofeld, 'That never happened when the Ashes were at stake'. He was right. As a sportswriter committed to the traditional side of the debate Blofeld pressed the point but was at least making a token effort at critical analysis – unlike some of the other English journalists. John Woodcock wrote in *The Times*, 'If history was indeed being made, it passed almost unnoticed'. And the *Daily Mail*'s Ian Wooldridge thought the game was 'like a battle fought with blank ammunition'. It's hard to tell whether these attitudes were based on prejudice or whether the game really was as hollow as they described. The empty stands wouldn't have helped. At this point the cricket punters were voting with their feet. WSC remained on a knife-edge.

And there was still a bit of fine-tuning to do. The camera work was given top marks – the cameramen, who at Kerry's Australian Open Golf could cover the high and lazy arc of a golf ball centre frame every time, were now learning to do the same with a million-mile-an-hour cricket ball suddenly slogged at an unexpected angle. But the sound was a bit of a problem. Cricketers, especially batsmen under pressure, can be pretty vocal and expletive. In the match Ian Chappell, never one for mild restraint, had batted for longer than anyone else for his 118 and throughout his innings had cried 'fuck!' to himself at various intervals – a poor shot, a near miss, a good shot cut off. It was a continuing problem. 'The count for the first season was something like thirteen shits, fourteen you bastards, three fucks and one cunt that got to air,' Crilly is quoted as saying. As head sound guy Colin Stevenson had to find a fix, Kerry knew if too much of this stuff ended up in Australia's living rooms he'd have the Broadcasting Tribunal all over him. Stevenson's solution was to reduce the number of microphones at each end (from four to two), to ride the sound with the fader and bring up other noises over the batsmen's voice.

The children of the revolution had now been at it nonstop for more than a year, working their over-worked days, pushing, prodding, arranging, innovating, doing extraordinary things for the first time, doing it against a backdrop of disapproval and enmity from entrenched powers and doing it all with Kerry riding their every waking moment. In this hothouse environment personality clashes and conflicts of style of administration were inevitable. As the pressure built each of the operatives had to find their own way of dealing with the stress. WSC had no template – it wasn't really like any other organisation that had ever existed. Half the team were sportsmen, or ex-sportsmen who knew cricket intimately, who had *lived* the game, who understood all its grand traditions and wondrous complexity. This was all about the game and how best to bring a fresh type of cricket to those punters out there who shared their love of it all and who might be willing to part with a few bucks to watch it. It was about wickets and players and fields and balls. The others were ruthless businessmen who knew pretty much nothing about the game but who recognised a startling new business opportunity when they saw one, entrepreneurs who knew the whole enterprise was not much more than an exercise in salesmanship. Who gives a flying fuck what colour ball we use? What are we selling? Cricket. How are we selling it? Sponsorships, TV ads, billboards – any way you like. Make us an offer.

On both sides of the internal divide, every one was an ego, every one bright, supremely competent, surefooted and used to getting his or her own way. For all his flaws of personality, Kerry was good at surrounding himself with the best and the brightest.

They were bound to clash, but they learned quickly how to contain damage, how to play the game. Asked about internal ructions, one member of the inner circle described another senior executive as a guy who spent his time, 'running round like a fucking chook without its head', but added, 'We didn't fight, we were too busy working'. In the main, professionalism kept a lid on the simmering tensions. Consiglieri John Cornell seemed to float above the fray and the maestro Richie Benaud, continuing the elegant style developed during his cricket captaincy days was seemingly able to force his will without getting anyone offside.

Still, with the build-up of tension and pressure and as the final days to the first critically important Supertest loomed, something had to snap. On 30 November, John Curtain, the guy charged with running the Country Cup matches, decided he'd had enough. The ostensible reason was the lack of cricket knowledge amongst many of the WSC administrators – in particular Vern Stone – and the fact that he'd been unable to get the proper assistance he needed. 'Too few people are left to do too much,' the *Sydney Morning Herald* quoted him as saying the morning after his resignation. He excluded Richie and Daphne Benaud from his spray, praising the 'incredible' amount of work they got through and how they were at it, toiling away thanklessly, seven days a week from dawn to midnight. Chris Forsyth says he got a typical Benaud memo the next day refuting the charge.

'You can tell the press,' it said, 'that I was under such tremendous pressure yesterday I played 18 holes of golf'.

The press sniffed blood in the water. If one of them had chucked it all in, were there others who might be about to do the same? Was it really all huggy and kissy inside the WSC tent or were these alpha guys secretly tearing each other apart? Reporters zeroed in on Forsyth as publicity head and he managed to hold them off with expertise and charm. Not too much later when a journalist quoted him in an uncomplimentary article about WSC – Forsyth had spoken on the condition of anonymity – Kerry sacked him. But after a few of the senior operators buttonholed Kerry, Forsyth found himself reinstated. Kerry was emulating his father who over the years had famously sacked and reinstated many *Daily Telegraph* staffers. Columnist Ron Saw is reputed to have been kicked off the paper *five* times by the old man, then gruffly told the following day he had his job back.

Curtain's resignation was a stumble, but small enough, and WSC soon righted itself. The pressure told in a more significant way with a major issue that polarised the executive team – the debacle over gate entry fees. Back in July, when the waters were calm and the course clear ahead, it had been decided that entry to WSC games would be set at $6 a day for adults and $2 for children, much more than the cricketing public were used to paying. In Sydney and Melbourne, punters were used to forking out two, three, four dollars for reserved seating. Various WSC administrators rumbled that $6 was way too high, especially for something that had never been tried before. Let's start low – at least as low as our competitors – and maybe build up to six bucks. But Kerry was adamant and so was the guy in charge of ticketing, Brian Treasure.

This decision simmered in there like the presence of some low-level radioactivity, sooner or later it was bound to go critical. And it did in November when the WSC turnstiles at last opened for business – and stayed horribly silent. The press was whingeing, reflecting the public's concern, and advance ticket sales to the first few WSC games were practically non-existent. Disaster threatened. Either WSC was a dud concept or the public had decided not to pay a $2 premium to see it – or both. The boil-over came when, inside the tent, the anti-$6 forces finally managed to convince Kerry to lower the price. That, at least, got rid of one problem. If the crowds still decided not to come, WSC was in significant trouble.

The crowds didn't come. At least they didn't come in sufficient numbers to make anyone think WSC was at last getting off the ground. The anxiously awaited first Supertest at VFL Park started off with disaster written all over it. To start off, in-form Australian batsman Ian Redpath had badly injured his ankle two days previously (he broke it in a game, jumping up and down celebrating that he'd just dismissed Clive Lloyd), and was out for a long spell. Only a few hundred people bothered being there for the first over of the first day. The crowd then built, but oh so slowly. Over the three playing days a crowd of 13,885 turned up. A bit over 4000 people a day in the 77,000 arena meant the cricketers out in the centre were staring at 73,000 empty seats. And it looked worse when you considered the last time these two teams met in Melbourne 85,000 people had been there – just for day one.

The West Indians went on to thrash the Australians in three days, leaving two whole days of nothing and chopping the gate takings off at the knees. But the game produced a timeless moment, the final dramatic seconds of day three. At 5 o'clock in the afternoon with one hour to play and the West Indies needing 45 to win, Andy Roberts, not known for his batting prowess, came in to join fellow tail-ender Deryck Murray and the two final batsmen prepared to face the terrible might of Ian Chappell's attack – Lillee, Pascoe, Walker. The game was all but over. For an hour Roberts and Murray ducked and weaved as the Australian fast bowlers, gloves off, gave them everything in the armoury. But single by nail-biting single the two men inched their way towards the magic 45 runs. They got agonisingly close – needing only four runs to win when close of play arrived at 6 pm. The umpires then decided to add an extra 45 minutes to get a result. Ray Bright was brought on and Andy Roberts carefully blocked five balls. With his eye in he stepped forward to the final ball of the over and won the game by smashing it for six.

Roberts' heroics weren't enough to save the match in the eyes of most of the press. The lack of spectators was what counted most. A lot of journalists missed the Roberts moment anyway. Having hung around for a day or so looking at the empty stands they decided on their editorial attitude then took off to their typewriters.

Still, Kerry kept his positive face to the world – this was the first of the Supertests, remember, massive crowds would have been nice, but they weren't really expected. This one was just to test our television coverage, etc. After the game those insiders who had argued to set the entry fees at $4 started making noises about maybe taking the ticket prices down even lower. But this didn't happen – it would have looked too much like panic.

The limited-over International Cup matches in Perth, Sydney and Melbourne were held with the crowds miserably haphazard at best. And just to remind the WSC players that they were usurpers, the Establishment kept up its harassment everywhere. Gideon Haigh quotes Vern Stone before the first Perth one-day game: 'It was the same stuff as usually happened,' Stone recalls, 'Mysteriously, people emerged to put parking tickets on cars. Police banned liquor going in to our ground while they were letting it into the WACA.' More of the same treatment Dennis Lillee got from Perth authorities back when hostilities had initially broken out.

WSC was hanging by its fingernails and its opponents settled in, watching closely, not wanting to miss the final fall. In the words of Eric Beecher in *The Cricket Revolution*, 'There was great interest in seeing whether the ship would continue to sink. Two limited over matches at Adelaide's sprawling Football Park the following weekend before more empty grandstands seemed to suggest it was still taking water at a rapid rate.'

The second Supertest between Australia and the West Indies at the Sydney Showground just before Christmas 1977 is the match that just might have been the initial spark, the first tiny but painful flare of something significant. It's a moment of utmost importance to the WSC insiders, every one of them still keen to bring it up and discuss its implications – a moment burned into their memories. Before this, the media all over the world had hammered the hollow 'exhibition match' theme and sports commentators had been trying to outdo each other in finding clever-dick ways to define WSC as insignificant cricket-lite. These hot shot cricketers are out there pretending to play cricket, but all they're doing is standing round the field trying to work out how best to spend their money. Where's the blood and guts of the old game, played by men of passion?

The unforgettable flash came in bright sunshine just after the tea break on 16 December 1977, day one of the Sydney Showground Supertest with David Hookes batting, Andy Roberts bowling and Richie Benaud commentating. Australia had been in all sorts of difficulties at five for 89 but had rallied. Wunderkind Hookes was on fire, stroking his way towards what looked like an inevitable century. At 81 he caught an Andy Roberts fast-rising killer ball flush in the face and the game went into surreal slow motion. Benaud's voice never sounded so elegantly otherworldly, 'He's hit him'. The impetus of Hookes' swipe at the ball took him around in a slow circle. He looked fine – then as the exquisite pain of a smashed jaw flashed through him he collapsed slowly to the turf. 'And he's in trouble,' said Benaud calmly.

With Andy Roberts standing nearby, cool-as-you-please, Hookes was helped off, spitting blood and holding a hand to the terrible double-fracture of his jaw and cheekbone. Kerry dashed down from the stands to the dressing room where the support staff had Hookes laid out on a table. Someone called for an ambulance but Kerry wasn't in any mood to hang around, 'Bugger the ambulance'. He bundled Hookes into the front seat of his Jaguar and roared off to St Vincent's Hospital, breaking the speed limit, screaming through red lights, crossing to the wrong side of the road. Hookes is reported to have been terrified. 'Slow down!' he screamed. 'I'm just trying to take your mind of your jaw,' said Kerry. 'Well, you're doing a bloody good job of it,' said Hookes. The next day doctors operated on his face and he was pronounced out of cricket for the next five or six weeks.

Kerry's instinctive actions that day were typical of a particular facet of his kaleidoscopic personality. He had to get one of his stars fixed as soon as possible, of course, but there was something in Kerry that reacted with visceral and immediate concern to hurt or discomfort in others. Those who knew him tell anecdotal tales of sudden and unexpected empathy coming from God knows where inside this big and brutal man. Helping strangers and friends. Maybe he was remembering his boyhood. He would turn warm, different, wanting to fix things, to make it all right again, the mean bully falling away to reveal someone who just wanted to help. Tony Greig once described him as 'soft as anyone's grandmother'. John Cornell tells of a trip to Perth with Kerry – they sat back, shoes off, talking cricket. When they landed Cornell says, 'for some reason my feet had swelled up and I couldn't get my shoes back on'. Kerry let the passengers off the plane and as the bemused Qantas staff looked on, knelt down on the floor at Cornell's feet and gently put his shoes on.

The significance of Hookes' broken jaw at one stroke tore away the appearance of artificiality in WSC. It was patently clear these guys weren't faking it or phoning it in. Andy Roberts, Lillee, Holding, Garner, Daniel, Snow and a few others almost as fast, weren't pissing around. Fast bowlers, a singular breed, have intimidation as their bread and butter. It's been estimated, given the speed of the ball and the length of a cricket pitch, that batsmen have about a third of a second to decide what to do with the ball coming at them. If batsmen are thinking this 150 kilometres per hour thing might destroy their cheekbone or their teeth they're sure as hell not thinking of their feet and where to place them, or their choice of shot. If they're not able to dig into instinct, short-circuiting the process of normal decision-making, then they're thinking survival, physical survival, and when that happens they duck and 'up periscope' with their bat, or use it as a

Top Australian cricketers (L–R) Ian Chappell, Jeff Thomson and Dennis Lillee in the dressing room, summer 1974–75. (Newspix / News Ltd)

Above (L–R) Greg Chappell, John Cornell and Dennis Lillee. (Courtesy of John and Delvene Cornell)

Left Paul Hogan with John Cornell and Delvene Delaney from *The Paul Hogan Show*. (Newspix / News Ltd)

Above Kerry Packer is introduced to the World Series
Cricket West Indies team by captain Clive Lloyd, 1977.
(*The Age*)

Below Four Australian cricket captains, 1977. (L–R)
Ian Chappell, Bill Lawry, Bob Simpson and Richie Benaud.
(*The Age*)

Above Kerry Packer batting for Australia Press XI vs England Press XI at Harrogate, England, 14 August 1977. (Newspix / News Ltd)

Above left Kerry Packer arriving at the High Court in London on 26 September 1977 at the start of his action against the Test and County Cricket Board. (David Ashdown / Keystone / Getty Images)

Below left WSC World captain Tony Greig in London, 30 September 1977, during the Packer case at the High Court. (Rob Taggart and Monti Spry / Central Press / Hulton Archive / Getty Images)

Top Kerry Packer's million-dollar World Series Cricket Australian team at Moorabbin Oval, Melbourne, 1977. BACK (L–R) Kerry O'Keefe, Ray Bright, Wayne Prior, Mick Malone, Ian Davis, Graham McKenzie, Len Pascoe, Rick McCosker, Rod Marsh, Ross Edwards, Dennis Lillee and Trevor Chappell. FRONT (L–R) Ashley Mallett, Gary Gilmour, Ian Redparh, Ian Chappell, Doug Walters, Greg Chappell, Richie Robinson, David Hookes, Max Walker and Bruce Laird. 16 November 1977. (Newspix / News Ltd)

Above Cricket pitch at VFL Park (now Waverley Park) being moved into position for use in World Series Cricket, October 1977. (Newspix / News Ltd)

Top left Kerry Packer amongst the crowd at a World Series Cricket match at VFL Park (now Waverley Park), Melbourne, 24 November 1977. (Central Press / Hulton Archive / Getty Images)

Top right Kerry Packer speaks to the press about the latest developments in World Series Cricket in 1977. (Hulton Archive / Getty Images)

Above World Series Cricket at the SCG under the new lights, 'Packers Cigars', 28 November 1977. The $1.4 million lights were switched on by chairman of the SCG Trust, Pat Hills. (Peter Leyden / Newspix / News Ltd)

Above World Series Cricket, Australia vs West Indies, 1 January 1978. Rod Marsh's catch off bowler Dennis Lillee (R) dismisses Viv Richards. (Newspix / News Ltd)

Above right Australia's Max Walker in action during the World Series Cricket match between Australia and the World XI at the Sydney Showground, 15 January 1978 (Julian Zakaras / *Sydney Morning Herald*)

Above far right David Hookes hits out at World Series Cricket on 13 February 1978. (*The Age*)

Ian Chappell wears
Australia's coloured
outfit for the first
time in the one-day
International against
the West Indies at the
SCG. 'It looks okay
but unfortunately
it's mostly white and
there is still a problem
of seeing the white
ball against the white
background,' he said.
(John O'Gready /
Sydney Morning Herald)

Top John Cornell (Abe Forsythe) and Delvene Delaney (Cariba Heine) in the TV mini series *Howzat! Kerry Packer's War*. (The Shot Enterprises / Natasha Blankfield)

Middle Tony Greig (Alexander England) and Greg Chappell (Damon Gameau) discuss the game in the change rooms following the Centenary Test in the TV mini series *Howzat! Kerry Packer's War*. (The Shot Enterprises / Natasha Blankfield)

Below An injured David Hookes (Richard Davies) is rushed to hospital by Kerry Packer (Lachy Hulme) during the second World Series Supertest at the Sydney Showground in the TV mini series *Howzat! Kerry Packer's War*. (The Shot Enterprises / Natasha Blankfield) shield – a sure recipe for disaster. Batting helmets, essential equipment just a short time later, didn't exist in early WSC, but lightning wickets did, and so did some of the fastest bowlers who ever existed. And WSC was selling itself as fast-paced adrenaline cricket, based largely on the entertainment value of quick bowling. Bishan Bedi's three short steps and spinning lollypops might have been excruciatingly clever and almost impossible to play, but they didn't have the terrifying impact of a thunderbolt from, say, Roberts or Holding or Lillee.

McCosker's smashed jaw in the Centenary Test had been held up as an example of a man putting himself in harm's way for his country in the finest tradition of the ancient and warlike game. Now here was Hookes, wired up and in pain just like McCosker, and no one was saying he did it for the money. Not any more. With the headlines and photographs and news footage of the incident came the first seeds of WSC legitimacy – sown in the minds of the public by Andy Roberts and David Hookes.

It would take some time for respect for WSC to grow, meanwhile the non-attendance continued as awful as

it could possibly be. Just before Christmas, a one-day
WSC match between the West Indies and the World,
some of the finest cricketers in the game going head to
head, was out-gated by the local Victoria versus NSW
Sheffield Shield game. Members of the press were chor-
tling. In the *Sunday Times*, Michael Parkinson noted,
'Mr Packer's problems with crowds'. He had seen, he
said, 'bigger attendances at the quarter finals of the
Barnsley District Shin-kicking competition'. The third
Supertest, held at Adelaide's Football Park over the New
Year drew an aggregate crowd of just over 15,000 people
– meanwhile the Third Test between the traditional
teams from Australia and India packed the MCG with
more than 82,000.

The official Australia versus India games over that
long summer were the bete noir for WSC and easily the
authorities' best and most effective weapon. The punters
were given a clear choice between traditional cricket and
the Packer circus and they let Kerry and his troops know
that, although they had no particular animosity to the
new stuff, they preferred real Test cricket.

The official Australian Test team mightn't have the
best players in the world, but it had an ace up its sleeve.
The ACB played their cards cleverly in recruiting an old
stager to their cause, former Australian captain Bobby
Simpson. Hey, WSC might have Benaud and Sobers,

but look who we got! At 41, Robert Baddeley Simpson was in that Benaud/Sobers category, highly respected not only by the world authorities but importantly also by Kerry and his cohort, a fine batsman, an outstanding slips fieldsman, bowler and smart cricket captain –pushy, confident of his own abilities, a man with a reputation for getting things done. He was also in the Clive Lloyd category, a stern sergeant-major who asked – demanded – a lot from his players and himself. Such was his reputation that he had even been one of the key figures Kerry chose to discuss his plans with at the very genesis of WSC (after a meeting or two they decided to go their own ways).

Simpson had reached the sunlit plains of cricket stardom, playing his first test in 1957 and retiring as Australian captain 11 years later with a solid reputation and a top Test score of 311 (in an Ashes match in 1964). He had settled into pottering about in hobby Grade cricket for Western Suburbs in Sydney but in October 1977 he was recruited by Parish and Steele, to much celebration and cheers from the Establishment side of the divide. Here was the old bull getting a second-string Australian team up to taking on the might of the Indian XI which, incidentally, boasted Gavaskar and Bedi. Although he hadn't played any sort of decent cricket for ten years, in his first game back he top scored (with 89) for Australia in the second innings of the Brisbane Test. He went on that summer to bang up 539 runs at an average of 53.9 and lead Australia to a 3–2 win over India.

With a man of Simpson's stature on board – the official Australian XI was known that summer and has been known ever since as 'Bobby Simpson's Eleven' – the authorities' counter-attack took on real force. Getting over the painful setback dished out by the High Court in London, the authorities were learning from WSC. Simpson and his quickly improving Australians hauled in the crowds while WSC languished. And following WSC's lead the ACB began a forceful promotion of its cricket, lobbying media executives, schmoozing journalists, hitting the airwaves with radio and TV promotions, accentuating the positive – look what we've got: 'Fair Dinkum Test Cricket'.

In a fine twist of history, like the Catholic Church split in the late fourteenth century that produced two Popes, the great cricket schism gave Australia two cricket captains. And, just like the other two, sooner or later Chappell and Simpson were going to attack each other. Simpson fired first, choosing an unlikely and highly unexpected theme – style.

The Australian Test cricketers of the so-called 'Chappell era' – under Ian followed by Greg – were not known for their sartorial splendour or their perfect manners.

They were known in parts as the 'Ugly Australians' and their reputation was as the untidy Hell's Angels of the cricket world. Nasty bastards. A tight gang of like-minded, long-haired killers who loved cricket, each other, and winning – in reverse order. They played hard cricket, they dressed as they pleased and if you didn't like it you could fucking well step outside (this, incidentally, was pretty much the reputation of the Australian XI for the next 25 years). But along came Bobby Simpson with his pre-Chappell-era attitudes and his insistence that his short-haired players carried themselves like gentlemen in ties, neatly pressed blazers and slacks. They repre-sented the great game and they were damn well going to look the part.

As Henry Blofeld has pointed out, 'There can have been few if any worse-behaved sides than those presided over by the two Chappells. A combination of thongs, shorts and shirts open to the navel, T-shirts, tracksuits and hardly ever a coat or blazer was the aggressive dress of the Chappell era. Punctuality was negotiable, the players did only what suited them, and the wishes of a succession of tour managers were ignored'. Blofeld was biased, of course, but he wasn't wrong.

In January 1978, Bobby Simpson saw this as the perfect target and let fly against the freewheeling style of Ian Chappell's T-shirted, trackie-dakked gang who sledged with abandon on the field and snarled at umpiring decisions, describing them as 'slobs'.

Ian Chappell, who had played Test cricket with Simpson, fired back immediately. 'Mudslinging,' he said, 'Simpson is being ridiculous and doing everything he can to downgrade the Packer series. It's the policy of the ACB to knock this series and Simpson is just carrying through that policy. As far as I'm concerned winning is the thing in cricket and it makes no difference whether you wear jeans and T-shirts off the field if you are comfortable'.

It was a clash of attitude – and one that's been around since sport was invented. Do dress codes and personal off-the-field discipline translate to a better performance on the field? Or is the sporting field a discrete place, a universe of its own, a closed system, and what you do off it doesn't count? One side of the debate insists on curfews and good behaviour and abstaining, the other side says if you turn up on time and play to the best of your outstanding abilities you can be a drugged-up home-grown serial killer if you like. One side says you are a role model (this has become the orthodox position in the past 20 years), the other side says maybe serial killer is going too far, but hey, 'winning is the thing'. The Chappell era players didn't get up to anything like the shenanigans of their children's peers – coked-up football players with girls in toilet cubicles three at a time – groupydom in the 1970s was characterised by a certain restraint and understanding of the rules – but the lads, and many of their international opponents, particularly the West Indians, were party people. Some claimed – and why wouldn't you believe them – that letting go completely got their mind off cricket and helped them focus so much better out there the next day.

The two sides of the timeless debate were personified in the two captains. Asked about it years later Ian Chappell replied, 'To me it's very simple. What do you need curfews for? Why do you need rules and regulations when you've got selectors? I don't give a shit what time a bloke stays up till, or what he does, if he makes runs and gets wickets then I'm fine. If he doesn't, he gets dropped. The players understand that'. He went on to say that Kerry did his best to enforce curfews and stiff regulations amongst his WSC players, but never quite managed it.

★

Hookes' smashed jaw was a tipping point in cricket history, the moment when batting helmets suddenly went from something contemplated only by pussies or scaredy-cats or bad batsmen, to becoming essential equipment not only for batsmen facing quick bowlers, but any fieldsman standing in close. There are a thousand claimants to the line that the players had gone through a hundred years of the game with special protection for their testicles but nothing for their brains. The comment is mostly attributed to girlfriends and/or wives. Just like men – protecting what's most important to them. McCosker's jaw had various players wondering – then Hookes' jaw did the rest. In the summer of 1977 the helmet was an idea whose time had come.

England WSC batsman Dennis Amiss is credited as the guy who first put on a real helmet. At first he wore his 'bonedome' as he called it, in the nets, getting used to it. Finally, in Adelaide in late November in a four-day game for the World against the West Indies, he stepped out onto the international stage to face the chuckling and the catcalls. The bonedome was a huge, spherical white and shiny thing, like a 1950s racing-driver crash helmet – something you might see on Sterling Moss or Juan Fangio – with a transparent visor at the front that he claimed was bulletproof. It had the makers' initials 'SP' in black print prominent at the front and it made him look top-heavy. SP stood for 'Saint Peter', initials of a British manufacturer of cricket equipment including batting mitts, which the players liked, and a white 'Flat Bat', which they hated.

'It's a prototype,' Amiss insisted, 'I'm testing it out. By the end of the season I hope to know exactly what is required and we'll make the necessary modifications'.

This crash helmet had a clear provenance. Amiss had reportedly got the idea of the big SP clunker when he saw England captain Mike Brearley at the crease wearing a strange-looking contraption on his head with thin fibreglass plates down each side to protect his temples. The conventional wisdom was that the temple was the most vulnerable part of the skull, a view you'd have trouble putting to McCosker or Hookes.

Brearley, in turn, got the idea from Tony Greig, in contact with a firm that manufactured protective head equipment for epileptics, who had made him a specially designed leather helmet, something like a boxer's helmet with a visor that stuck out the front and a nifty little chin-strap. He used this proto-headgear, he said, to ready himself against fast-paced bowling, wearing it in the nets as he practised whipping bouncers away from his face.

Amiss made his helmet debut three weeks *before* Hookes jaw was smashed and during those three weeks he faced nothing more than mild interest and bemusement. But with Hookes in hospital everyone wanted to know where they could get one. They were in luck. Amiss' wife, who arrived in Australia from the United Kingdom on the very day of Hookes' injury, brought four helmets with her, and 48 hours later Kerry organised for a sample lot of the helmets to be flown to Australia from Saint Peters in Birmingham. Australian helmet-makers, who had been sniffing round the idea anyway, got in on the act quickly, figuring that the things were only going to get popular with the players if the aesthetics were right. The SP specials might protect the players' faces and heads but they were too heavy, the plastic visors scratched and the players complained they couldn't move freely while wearing one. And they made the players look as if they'd just got out of a Formula One car. Something like a polo helmet with a chin guard became the template and gradually the designs were tweaked.

Batsmen came slowly to the idea. They had, after all, been facing killer balls aimed at their brains for their whole careers, but in dribs and drabs they took up this aspect of the WSC revolution. After the second Supertest, Amiss, Greig and Barry Richards wore their lumpy SPs as a matter of course, belting a number of fine innings. They were soon joined by McCosker (of course), Knott, Mushtaq, Zaheer, Langer and Ian Davis. 'People would give you strange looks and a few bowlers were interested in knocking it off,' said Davis.

They sure were. For their part the fast bowlers just couldn't help themselves. Instead of a head of hair or a coloured cap, down the end there was a fucking great white thing to aim at. It couldn't have looked more like a target if it had concentric red circles painted on it. The batsmen found themselves smacking balls away from their heads, looking for all the world as if they didn't want to get their shiny new crash hats dented. In the fifth Supertest at Gloucester Park in Perth in January 1978, Dennis Lillee sent down a bouncer to Tony Greig which lifted alarmingly late. Greig did his best to get out of its way but – Klang! The sound reverberated round the oval and the fieldsmen killed themselves laughing. Lillee at the end of his run, grinned at Greig and tapped his head with a finger – gotcha! Greig smiled back, turned and waggled his arse at Lillee.

Here again was the divide. Traditionalists, particularly in England, were unimpressed by this behaviour and aghast that cricketers were going onto the field in lumpy headgear looking like spacemen. Helmets were seen as yet another unsightly insult to the game, like coloured clothing or the white ball. It was just another example of how WSC didn't give a damn about the subtle traditions of the game. English batting legend Colin Cowdrey and others tut-tutted that fast bowling and the over-use of bouncers was the problem here. The solution wasn't funny hats, it was in cutting back the number of bouncers allowed each over. And anyway, bouncers or no bouncers, batsmen should face bowlers just the way they always had, with skill and courage, their bare heads in God's sunshine or in a cloth cap. The batsmen weren't listening to them, of course, and the helmet innovation of the summer of 1977–78 went on to conquer the cricketing world. Primary school kids, wanting to look like their gladiatorial heroes, now don their plastic helmets before striding proudly to the centre.

★

Play continued on both sides, the first three Supertests clashing directly with the Bobby Simpson matches – and traditional cricket had easily the best of it. But WSC was new and flexible and making it up as it went along. When the third Supertest in Adelaide in December 1977 failed to pull in the punters Adelaide was then wiped off the WSC map. Not going *there* anymore. Kerry made the decision to concentrate on Sydney and Melbourne (with Brisbane thrown in). 'Why do we need to be everywhere?' he said, 'It's only the ACB that needs to play a Test in every capital city. We'll stick to where the people are'.

The next game, the fourth Supertest between Australia and the World at the Sydney Showground (won by the World) on 14–18 January 1978 pulled in an aggregate crowd of 36,424. Not all that good but twice that of the Adelaide debacle. That fixed that.

WSC morale began building. But in the fifth Supertest at the end of January, only 13,562 Perth punters arrived through the gates and dark despair set in again. Those Perth cricket-lovers who did bother turning up though, saw another shining moment in cricket history when the two Richards legends, Barry and Viv – the white South African and the black West Indian – came together at the crease and decided to outdo each other. (One commentator noted helpfully, 'Barry Richards is the one in the helmet'.)

As soon as this pair of timeless champions, batting for the World team against Ian Chappell's men, got up a head of steam Australia was never in the game. Viv banged up 177 while Barry welcomed himself back to the big time with 207. And just for good measure Gordon Greenidge, Barry's opening partner, chipped in with 140. Despite a classic 174 from Australia's Greg Chappell, the World won by an innings and 73 runs.

This match was one that highlighted a growing animosity, even enmity, between Ian Chappell and Tony Greig, delicately referred to in official WSC publicity as 'intense rivalry'. It was widely known and reported with relish by sections of the Press, that the two captains had a powerful dislike of each other through the WSC years. Some journalists put it down as a simple marketing ploy – here they were, both highly visible, both hard men, acting like a pair of world class heavyweight boxers, leaping at each other at the weigh-in, only to declare their fondness for each other in post-match interviews.

But it wasn't like that. It was real. 'I must say I was the bloody instigator,' says Chappell, 'He was only responding'. Neither man can, or bothers to, remember the absolute genesis of this long-term clash, but both speak about it as authentic hostility. The pair had already taken captain's competitiveness to new heights in the Ashes clashes of 1975, provoking each other, exchanging insults on the field. A year later, with both men inside the WSC tent, Chappell recalls initially resenting the fact that Greig, who had a lot of outside-cricket responsibilities (his promotion of Kellogs, Waltons and so on), was neglecting his cricket training.

'Kerry was agitating for training and guys not training hard enough', he says, 'I'm thinking well that's a bit hypocritical. Who's this fucker earning extra money and he's not practising with the team and we're getting shit for not training hard enough'.

The two men kept up their war throughout the first WSC season and it built into the second. Their flash of peak drama came after the final SCG Supertest in February 1979, lost by Australia in a snarly moment when with the World needing two runs to win, Ian Chappell brought himself on to bowl and hurled the ball for four wides. It was Chappell's custom to visit the opposition's changing room after a match. 'If we got beaten I'd go to the opposition dressing room and say well played to the team,' he says, "Well played guys, well played".'

On this day he went into the World dressing room, long-neck bottle of beer in hand (the protocol was you always took your own, you didn't go and congratulate the other team and start drinking their beer). The moment he walked in he was spied by Greig, who told him he was not wanted and he could 'fuck off'. Chappell says he replied, 'Well, if you want me out of the dressing room you fucking throw me out'. He then proceeded to shake hands with, congratulate, everyone in the room – except Greig. 'I got to Greigy and I didn't put my hand out. I just said "your team played well again".'

Greig remembers it differently – Chappell came in, moved around the room congratulating the players, finally getting to Greig, who graciously put out his hand to shake. 'But he refused to shake hands with me,' he says. Chappell then left the room, Greig says, but when he returned a short time later, 'I picked up the bat and said, mate, you're not welcome. Get out of here'. Chappell had returned to the change room in anger because a journalist reported to him that Greig had described him as 'a bad loser'.

Despite the fact that these men have become friends in the ensuing years that moment still burns for Tony Greig. 'I've never played a game of sport ever in my life where I haven't shaken hands with the opposition,' he says, 'At the end of the day, no matter what your situation is, you shake hands at the end of a game of cricket'.

Following the WSC years, having hung up their boots, the two men went on to be key commentators in the Nine Network's coverage of international cricket – alongside Richie Benaud, Bill Lawry and various other guest commentators – spending hours, days, weeks, locked in commentary booths together, sharing taxis and cars at match venues, eating together, appearing shoulder to shoulder at functions. There is no way such an intimate, popular and successful professional relationship could have continued if these guys had kept up the animosity. Asked about the melting of the freeze, Chappell says, 'I think we both just grew a brain'.

'After a year or two of commentary I suddenly thought one day, fucking hell this is silly, we're going to be working together and it could be for a long time. It's bloody silly for me to go on with this. I never ever said anything to Tony but I just sort of shelved it from then on … And there hasn't been a problem since.'

Greig's take is that they both got 'older and wiser'. 'But', he says, 'I will never, ever, accept the fact that there was any excuse for him not to shake hands'.

★

The magic moments of superlative Supertest dramas – Hookes' jaw, Roberts' six to win the first Supertest and the sublime spectacle of the two great Richards batting together – made for more misery in the WSC camp. Despite the quality of the cricket they were putting up, the quality of the cricketers on show, the innovations and the millions spent, the crowds were staying home. Cricket had never seen anything quite like this, but it was *just not working*. The Supertests were super indeed. Super-duper. Super-sized. Nothing had been left to chance. But still something was wrong.

And that was a large part of the problem. The WSC Supertests were the cricket equivalent of those $150 million movies that have everything going for them, everything big and gorgeous, perfectly put together, overpaid megastars on screen huger than life, the best camerawork, the best sound, the best overpaid directors, the product marketed, promoted, pre-sold, publicised and advertised within an inch of its life. And yet we can sit there feeling there must be more to the experience than this. We can witness flashes of brilliance and expertise, knowing we're supposed to be blown away by this grand extravaganza but feeling somehow there's a critical element missing. It's dramatic, to be sure, impressive, yes highly, but sometimes we just want to get out of there and watch a down and dirty little indie.

Kerry's improvement on Test cricket, giving it gloss and sheen, removing all semblance of the fusty and the used, making it somehow more accessible and more easily digestible was fine on paper – just look at all those famous names! But no matter how Supertests were packaged – paradoxically the more they were packaged – the more his enemies were happy to stick to their point. Sometimes the old steakhouse with its classic mixed grill and its retro old-school familiarity is enough. Tradition might be championed by reactionary types whose arteries are hardening and whose worldview is that of your parents, or, worse, their parents, but it's worked for a long time and it'll keep working as long as we have collective memory. The anti-WSC forces had trouble articulating their hatred for what Kerry was doing to their game, content to hammer on in a pouting froth about the terrible damage and the breaking of convention. In this context they were saying yesterday is better than tomorrow.

The cricketing public listened to what the old guard said and, lo and behold, they decided the old guard was right. Deep down, unconsciously, the punters didn't want to let go of something that had not only served them well over the years but had somehow been important. WSC pushed and prodded, beckoned, dangled its Supertest superstar carrots, did its jangling razzle-dazzle dance and the public, smiling that smile you give the guy in the park with the raincoat and the lollypop, politely backed off. You can lead a horse to water… And Super – from the word 'superior'– isn't always.

As it turned out the people didn't need Super Tests because they already had Tests. Bobby Simpson and his young and inexperienced official Australian XI were courageously fighting the Indian team in Test matches that had all the classical hallmarks of the best of the grand game. Test crowds that summer broke records for Australian/Indian Test matches in Australia. These games worked as well if not better than they always had, and the Australian public knew it. All innovation, in art or food or design or architecture or sport, you name it, is up against the irrefutable maxim – it's hard to beat the classics.

At this point in the WSC narrative the cricket gods smiled on Kerry and his gang. By fate, or luck, they had invented something new the cricketing public decided it *did* want. At VFL Park over three steamy nights in January 1978, WSC and the Australian public coalesced, both recognising that here was the true heart of the revolution. They came together over floodlit cricket.

It was a major turning point for WSC – that strange milestone in the hero's journey when he knows there's maybe, just maybe, a chance that he's not going to die. The initial untelevised blind shot at night cricket had come on 14 December at VFL Park with a 40-over match between Ian Chappell's Australians and Tony Greig's World team. Six and a half thousand people (exactly 6442 – a WSC record at the time) turned up mid afternoon and stayed through, cheering with delight when the huge lights came on at dusk. This was a tester for the new white ball – the old red one disappeared in the night sky and made catching lofted drives almost impossible – and a tester for night cricket in general. At half-time, the dinner break in the game, Kerry and John Cornell arrived by helicopter just as they had on that long-ago night when they first saw the field being chewed to bits by footballers. What they saw beneath the bright festive lights were kids gambolling all over the ground, mums and dads with picnic hampers and Eskys and Thermoses, and what they heard was the happy public buzz of cricket followers voting in favour of the revolution.

It wasn't just a one-off. At the next day–nighter under the blessed VFL Park lights on 24 January 1978, the 6442 record was completely blitzed. Five and a half thousand people arrived for the first ball at 3.30 in the afternoon and this had grown to over 18,000 by the time the lights came on, to more cheering. And they kept coming. By the time the game finished at nearly midnight, 24,636 had paid their money to witness the new spectacle. This flood of families kept up for the next two nights.

The press went nuts. Even those journalists who had worked extra hard to give Supertests a hard time came across with effusive compliments. Caught up by the party mood at the ground, feeling in their stomachs the old excitement of something special at the cricket, they went looking for warm superlatives. 'Just as the sun seemed to be setting on World Series Cricket's first dis-aster-filled season, someone turned on the lights,' wrote Eric Beecher, 'In a reprieve of enormous proportions the WSC organisers watched in amazement for three heady nights as more than 50,000 people poured into VFL Park. Night cricket had arrived to save WSC from almost certain death'.

'The crowd brought the VFL Park to life and the game itself provided splendid entertainment,' wrote Henry Blofeld, 'The atmosphere was gladiatorial, and the cricket as much as anything a night out for the young and the curious ... While the presentation and the commentary had seemed contrived during the five-day Supertests they both now matched the occasion'.

On that initial visit to VFL Park back in May and in the days following Kerry and Cornell had honed for themselves the cultural and geographic basis to the WSC manifesto. Why copy the Poms with their cool British Isles weather and their longer days? Let's make a new kind of cricket work for the fiery summers of Gond-wana. Here was their dream coming true.

Blofeld went on to note that day–night cricket might 'fulfil a social need in Australia if not elsewhere. It has a number of pluses. It is much more comfortable for spectators to watch in the cool of the evening than in temperatures which may be into three figures in the day-time; there is the instant excitement of one-day cricket, with the certainty of a result by the end of play; and as presented by Packer it made spectacular entertainment'.

WSC's prophesy that women would come to the cricket came wonderfully to fruition. The traditionally male game was now invaded by the new 1970s woman, the *Cleo* reader Kerry and Ita Buttrose had unearthed, attracted by the sporting spectacular and the fact that this type of cricket was essentially made for families. But a new dimension had been added to cricket – glamour. In the past international cricketers had tended to look a bit like your father, or your Uncle Percy, but not anymore. The beautiful gods of the game, players such as Dennis Lillee, Viv Richards, Imran Khan and David Hookes became pin-ups, sex symbols, and women flocked through the WSC turnstiles in unheard of numbers. Kerry's all-important TV-ad demographics widened beautifully and another box was ticked on the WSC wish list.

Kerry, happy man, held a press conference where, conveniently ignoring the wounded Supertests, he told reporters he'd always known his cricket was going to work. It had taken a bit longer than he figured and it had cost a stack more, and he'd copped a lot more opposition than he'd been expecting, but all in all things had turned out fine and the bad days were behind him. He was asked what he thought of the positive reaction to the VFL Park games. 'Fantastic, obviously,' he said. He knew he'd landed a body blow to his opposition.

For their part they chose to ride with the punch. The ACB held an immediate three-day full conference and decided on the 'me too' tactic, letting the press know that they'd been quietly planning their own cricket under lights.

'The Australian Cricket Board will give consideration to all aspects of the game in what we feel is our progressive administration,' said Bob Parish, 'This will include consideration to the introduction of night cricket'.

WSC's reaction to this sudden announcement was What!? Kerry remembered them describing night cricket as 'absurd' and 'a circus act' when he first announced it and Richie Benaud, in his usual dry style said, 'As a journalist of 21 years standing I know a world scoop when I see one and the story that the Australian Cricket Board has for some time had night cricket on the drawing board was a beauty'.

With his jaw still wired, two weeks after getting it smashed, David Hookes returned to the nets, understandably having nightmares of that terrible ball from Roberts. His doctors would have had him arrested if they'd known he was facing 140 kilometre per hour balls while the bones in his face were still unmended. But he forced himself, as these men do, and made a hesitant comeback in January in a Country Cup game in Hamilton, Victoria, a rural oval tucked well out of the limelight. The first critical ball he faced, on a very dicey pitch – the single ball he had to overcome to begin his healing process – came from the hand of speedster Michael Holding and was a looping slow full toss on leg stump – a ball Holding later said he would not have delivered if the game had been a Test match. But Hookes got to it easily, patted it away for a single and when he arrived at the bowler's end, caught up with Holding and thanked him. 'He just smiled,' Hookes said, 'it was the only freebie I got in two seasons'.

In February 1978, a few weeks after his wires were removed, in the International Cup limited-over semifinal, wearing a helmet for the first time, Hookes walked out onto the same ground where he'd been injured to confront not only the fastest bowlers in the world but his own internal demons. He got rid of his nemesis, Andy Roberts easily enough, hooking him for two huge sixes, but the internal, psychological damage was harder to shake. A year later the trauma was still affecting his cricket. 'I suppose I'd buried it a bit when I came back after Andy hit me the year before,' he told Gideon Haigh, 'but in New Zealand the pitches were so bad I started to get flashbacks about the ball he'd hit me with. He wasn't even there and in fact after a while it didn't matter who was bowling. The spinners could be on – and I'd see that ball again. And then I'd get out'.

The end of the first strange and bumpy season came

with the sixth Supertest at VFL Park between Australia and the World on 9–13 February 1978. After that game, won by the Australians by 41 runs – after Greg Chappell banged up 246 not out in the first innings and Dennis Lillee took five for 82 – the players had repaired to the 'Noise Room', a spartan bar with a loud jukebox in the basement of the Old Melbourne, the venue of choice for winding down after a match. This was the season's wrap party, where the pressures of months of living the new and the unknown, paradoxically in the bright lights of the media, could be put aside for a few hours. The Noise Room was where the cricketers could mix and play music and drink, and they proceeded to do a lot of all three. Flights out of there had been booked and every mother's son was looking forward to getting home. The guys moved about each other, remembering, congratu-lating, commiserating, farewelling. Kerry, a life-long non-drinker, was there mixing happily with his players with the usual glass of Coke or Fanta or just water in his hand. At times like this the players often mischievously tried to get the Boss to join them in a beer. Kerry would politely decline. Kerry's non-drinking was at odds with his hard man, wharfie demeanour – it didn't quite fit the character.

There are various versions out there in anecdotal gossip-land of why he never drank, what prompted him to be a teetotaller while mixing in a culture and at a time in history when alcohol was everywhere. One story is that old Sir Frank promised him a hot sports car on his twenty-first birthday if he didn't drink. Kerry took his father up on it and called in the debt as soon as he turned 21. The story says Sir Frank welched on the deal by giving him a second-hand sedan, but Kerry continued to stay off the grog. Another tale is told of Kerry as a passenger in a horrific highway car accident. The driver, a friend, had been drinking heavily. The horror burned into young Kerry and he swore off alcohol forever. The third story says teenage Kerry went out on the tiles with a few mates one night and he drank a whole bottle of gin (sometimes it's vodka). When he woke up the next morning he felt how he never wanted to feel again in his life. So he made sure he didn't. The truth could be any one or any combination of these, but it hardly matters. Although a committed teetotaller all his life, Kerry always took great pride in selecting the very best wines and champagnes for his guests and friends, but after that initial sommelier's sip he continued with something else.

That night in the hot and crowded Noise Room, Dennis Lillee, who had just taken his remarkable 5–82 but was struggling with a gradually worsening ankle injury, moved up to his captain and put out his hand.

'Dennis came over to me,' says Ian Chappell, 'and

started to make something that sounded to me like a retirement speech, this and that and whatever else, and he put his hand up and said shake me by the hand'.

'I said, "I don't shake medium pacers by the hand, mate, I only shake fast bowlers by the hand".'

Whack! Lillee plunged his fist into Chappell's stomach. 'Now shake my hand,' Lillee muttered. Chappell, after managing to straighten up, came back with more of the same. 'I don't shake hands with medium pacers.'

'Banged again,' grins Chappell, 'Three times he hit me. Anyway, after the third time he said, "Fuck you, I'll come back next season and I'll get more fucking wickets than anybody else in World Series Cricket". Which is exactly what he did'.

Chappell says his direct insult to the mightiest of fast bowlers was a motivational tactic. The greatest insult to a fast bowler is, of course, to call him a medium-pacer. 'To motivate Lillee,' says Chappell, 'you needed to set him some impossible task, something that apparently couldn't be done, or at least had never been done in history. You could tell him no Western Australian has ever taken five wickets at the SCG. And he'd say, "Well, we'll fucking see about that".'

Chappell says he dumped his insult on Lillee because he knew Lillee was feeling he wasn't bowling up to the stratospheric level of achievement he always set for himself and that it would 'annoy the shit out of him'.

'It did, and it got the result that probably we both wanted.' Lillee came back the following season faster, cleverer, fitter, after spending time in training with 71-year-old Austin 'Ocker' Robertson Senior – his friend Austin Robertson's father – who had been a world-class sprinter in his young days, known in the 1930s as 'the fastest man alive'. He taught Lillee the arcane craft of the very fast runner and Lillee, gifted athlete that he was, picked it up with ease. By the end of the following Australian winter he was well over his Noise Room funk and ready to put his name back into lights and into history.

The official break-up party was held at Melbourne restaurant, Lazar's, where the whole WSC band, players, administrators and everyone else, gathered to do it in style. By this time the aura of Kerry the terrifying squillionaire businessman had dissipated for his players and they were seeing him fondly, as a tough figure who not only knew what he was doing but seemed to enjoy the ride. They called him 'The Boss', impressed by the fact that he thought as they did, unlike the authorities they had been dealing with all their sporting lives. Here was a guy who was one of them. 'I thought he was a great guy,' Gary Gilmour is quoted as saying. 'He'd eat with us, drink with us, come to practice and bowl to you and dive around the field. He was a sportsman really, a competitor'.

'Packer had been everywhere,' wrote Gideon Haigh, 'joining practices, mowing outfields, opening his house to players who made use of his tennis court and swimming pool'.

The players enjoyed Kerry's wide open hospitality. Apart from the fact that he relished being surrounded by sportsmen, he was a generous and fascinating host, a magnet, a massive spinning planet, dragging friends and acquaintances into his ever-changing, whimsical orbit. Kerry soaked up experiences and wanted to share them, always with the latest gadget or device – the best sound equipment, the biggest TV, the earliest mobile phone (as big as a house brick with a metal antenna that had to be pulled up). The fastest cars. In London with Tony Greig during the High Court case, Greig and Kerry visited a Jaguar showroom to look over the Jaguar XJS, at the time the last word in sophisticated and dangerously fast motoring. Kerry, impressed, asked what colour they came in. Told there were five different colours, he ordered one of each (he gave four away to key executives).

WSC insiders tell the story of how a friend of Kerry's who owned a property bordering on Ellerston, used to wait for Kerry near Scone in his Ferrari and the two men would race home. The neighbour always won, so Kerry, infuriated, arranged for racing driver and fast car expert Kevin Bartlett to special his Jaguar, fitting it with some kind of terrifyingly huge motor. It was so big the front bonnet had to be hammered out with a power bulge you could hardly see over. There's no record of whether Kerry beat his neighbour in the next race – probably not. As soon as he collected his new monster, Kerry decided to take it for a test drive to Canberra. He was roaring along when he noticed a hitchhiker by the side of the road and picked him up. The kid was a young English backpacker, so Kerry, still driving at nightmare speed, quizzed him on WSC. It was a scene out of *Fear and Loathing in Las Vegas*. As one WSC exec tells it, 'The kid's sitting back in his seat, shitting himself, wondering who on earth he's run into. And suddenly the motor blows up'.

Smoke pouring from the bonnet of the Jaguar, the backpacker standing well clear, Kerry whipped out his housebrick phone and made a call. A short time later the Channel 9 helicopter landed beside them. Kerry loaded the now bewildered kid into the chopper and they flew to Canberra where a shiny limo was waiting on the tarmac. 'Where are you going?' asked Kerry. The kid was duly dropped off in style at the YMCA.

Unsleeping, restless, questing, *interested*, Kerry made his way through life, starting in the 1970s when he first began to feel his power, on a blitz of new experiences and adventurous campaigns that left his associates breathless. Like Alexander or Charlemagne or Henry VIII, he'd take off on some mad idea expecting his retinue not only to keep up, but to be as fascinated by the ride as he was. Once travelling to a WSC game by helicopter he turned to the pilot and asked, 'Are these things as safe as light aircraft?' The pilot, a long-term employee named Geoff Longland, told him yes, as a matter of fact, they're much safer. Kerry wanted to know how that could be – surely if something happens to the huge rotor blades, the thing just plummets to the ground. No, he was told, that's not the problem, it's only if the little rotor at the back is damaged that it's all over. 'So,' said Kerry, 'you can turn off the big motor and just glide'.

'Absolutely,' said Longland.

'Okay,' said Kerry. 'Turn the fuckin' thing off'.

In the back of the chopper were John and Delvene Cornell, listening to the hair-raising conversation. Cornell says he immediately stepped in. 'I said hold it a second, Kerry, I've got the crown jewels back here. (Delvene was pregnant at the time.) Let's leave the demonstration till when you're on your own.'

Kerry wasn't listening, 'Don't be a sook, son'. He ordered Longland to go ahead. He switched off the power, idled the engine, and sure enough, to Kerry's delight, the chopper wafted down and they landed safely at VFL Park.

Life was a lollyshop. Kerry had the money, the home-spun curiosity and the motivation to indulge his every whim. He gambled a vast fortune in the world's best casinos and racetracks. He played golf (good golf) and had a world-class course built at Ellerston. He played polo and later had top polo fields established on his properties in England and Australia. He sailed yachts. He played tennis. He went scuba-diving and deep-sea fishing. He once invited a bunch of his friends and exec-utives to Ellerston to see his latest toys – six ultra-light aircraft. Everyone had to have a go. The others, with Kerry yelling encouragement, got the spidery things up in the air, did a low, slow and gingerly arc round the take-off area, then landed with a sigh of relief. Kerry, scoffing, took off, headed into the sky… and kept going – disappearing over some hills. The others waited, but he never returned. So they jumped into a 4WD and went off looking for him, locating him out in the middle of a paddock. He'd almost run out of fuel but had managed to land without killing himself.

He had guns, many guns, and delighted in blasting away. Bruce Francis recalls a fine Saturday morning in Kerry's home in Sydney's Bellevue Hill with Kerry's wife Ros plus John and Delvene Cornell and Austin Robertson. Out in the backyard young James and some of his schoolmates were practising against the bowling machine. Delvene, seeing the brace of weapons in the room, asked Kerry if he was a good shot. 'Pick a spot on that tree and I'll show you how good I am,' said Kerry.

Ros stepped in, 'Please Kerry, not that tree. It took us days to get the bullet out last time'.

No problem. Kerry selected a huge 450 elephant gun. 'This'll go right through'. He cleared the kids from the yard and blasted a massive hole straight through the tree.

★

As that first critical summer came to a close and the exhausted players flew home to put their feet up for a short time, the WSC executives had a chance to settle back and take stock. What had worked? What was not working? Where did we go wrong? What did we do right? What needs to change? What did we get this summer – four, maybe five, out of ten? Next summer with a few tweaks and finetuning we can double that – then we're fine. As Kerry pointed out at the end-of-season WSC party, 'We were amateurs this year. Next year we're going to do it properly'.

Even now when Kerry spoke to the press he mentioned the inevitability of compromise and how he was all for it, and Tony Greig echoed his sentiments. But while they talked this talk, the hard line they'd chosen against the ICC and the ACB ever since the High Court win continued. Kerry kept insisting he was doing his best to open communications with the Establishment, but he wasn't really – his position was strong enough for him to hold out. As for the boards, they were in no mood to chase him, sitting in their wood-panelled bunkers snipping at each other, playing a waiting game, not averse to ending the war but not wanting to be seen to fold. Hostility and distrust continued. Compromise plans were mooted, but they were always 'unofficial'. Every time one of these made the press journalists plumped for action. Hearing the whisper of one stillborn effort involving the ICC, *London Times* correspondent John Woodcock wrote, 'Now is the time for the Board to make a move. They can bargain from a position of strength; they can cut down the bloodshed; they can cleanse the air. For the good of cricket something must be tried … it may mean a lot of dismounting from high horses'.

But no one was willing to do that. If either side in the first few months of 1978 had been legitimately wanting an armistice there's no doubt one could easily have been arranged. It didn't happen. And this was partly because Kerry, looking towards WSC's second season

– the 1978–79 summer in Australia – probably had a sneaking glimpse of possible total victory.

★

Not long after Kerry, as Chris Forsyth put it, 'took a look at the $7 million worth of WSC bills', WSC brought in a new and canny operator in the form of businessman Andrew Caro to lead its 'Governing Committee'. Caro, an Englishman who had moved to Australia and headed household goods manufacturer Reckitt and Colman, came in as managing director and proceeded to tuck the past turbulent year behind the organisation, distancing himself from what he saw as the ad hoc decision making of 1977. Corporate memory of a certain amount of chaos wouldn't do anyone any good, he figured, it was time to look forward and take this thing, such as it was, into calm and decisive waters. Time to take it onto more corporately solid ground. 'My credentials,' he wrote in 1979, were that 'I love cricket, have played it badly for 35 years both in England and in Australia. I was the Managing Director of World Series Cricket for its second full year of operation. I had no involvement in the first near-disastrous season'.

Once his appointment was formalised Caro didn't

mess around. Things were falling into place, small victories and friendly decisions started going WSC's way. First came the SCG, the new 12-member board putting out the welcome mat, chairman Pat Hills announcing that next summer eight WSC games would be played at the ground over 17 days. Playing on Establishment home turf not only gave WSC another small, warm victory but had the extra fillip of giving WSC more legitimacy in the eyes of the public. With night cricket clearly the way ahead it was necessary to have more grounds with floodlights like VFL Park. WSC money was put aside to cover this and Caro targeted the SCG, signing a deal with Pat Hills to erect six huge light towers. Despite howls of outrage, Neville Wran's government fast-tracked them and the cricket ground board insisted on paying for them. 'Fine,' thought Caro, 'that just saved us a cool million bucks.' Next came a deal for use of the Gabba in Brisbane. Yes, we'll take that one. What else you got?'

What else was the Adelaide Oval. Word came from Adelaide that Sir Donald Bradman and his fellow trustees of the South Australian Cricket Association (SACA) had decided to offer the ground to WSC. The Don and his fellow board members, strong-armed by a furious ACB, had earlier rejected WSC offers for use of the glorious oval. Eric Beecher described WSC's cheeky approach to the SACA as 'a little like Hitler asking Churchill for use of British airstrips during World War Two'. Now here was Bradman knocking on WSC's door delivering the wonderful ground and wanting to talk money. Meetings were held and Kerry found himself in a position he would have thought idyllic a year ago, but yawning at the offer. Who needs the Adelaide Oval? It had already been decided to concentrate on the better crowd possibilities of the Eastern seaboard. The South Australians were told thanks but no thanks.

The other fresh recruit was a new press supremo, a young whiz-kid from Sydney radio station 2GB, Bill Macartney, a friend of John Cornell's. Confident, charming, Macartney was seemingly tailor-made for the job, slotting straight in, energetically out there wrangling the press, pushing, cajoling, threatening, giving WSC a new in-your-face inevitability. Cricket writers on a slow day would find Macartney right there, giving them the inside latest. Previously hard to avoid, WSC was now everywhere.

It was clear WSC had now grown from a small and poisonous intruder in the house of cricket into an organisation with the size and power of any of its national opponents. No longer were the cricketers 'rebels' or WSC players part of a 'breakaway group', the Establishment and WSC were now equally matched. Kerry and his coterie knew they had passed the point of no return, having come this far they would simply keep forging aggressively, optimistically, ahead. One thing for sure, they weren't going away. As Henry Blofeld put it, 'by April 1978 (Kerry) and his WSC had become an established fact of life in the cricket world'.

Kerry had succeeded in splitting cricket down the middle. The cricket debate had polarised the press and the public to such an extent you were either for WSC or against it - either you wanted Kerry chased off with his tail between his legs or you were keen to see the old men of the game getting what was coming to them.

But whatever your position there's no doubt you were looking at a revolution and the noise of battle outside was now being heard loudly in the hallowed halls and trophy-lined corridors. 'Emergency' meetings had done no good. Lofty prounouncements were sounding increasingly hollow. Some sections of the press, once overwhelmingly on side, were wavering, sports journalists taking sides and digging in. Sniping between cricket writers, administrators and true believers on both sides became increasingly bitter. Kerry knew he was losing money, but so was everyone else. Numbers through the gates were dwindling, the national boards' incomes were in trouble, yet every board was being forced to pony up for the ICC's $320,000 legal bill. Bobby Simpson's XI went off to play tests in the West Indies with both the ACB and the WICBC knowing they'd both be taking a financial haircut. In the Fifth Test at Sabina Park in Jamaica the crowd rioted on the final day and the match was abandoned.

The view was desolate wherever you looked. Each side had its lawyers going over press comments with a fine-toothed comb and writs for libel and defamation were flying. One senior Establishment operative insisted his phone was bugged. And it got worse. The effect of WSC's continued, relentless pressure on its opposition meant the Establishment, unused to this type of gloves-off cage-match brawling, was striking out wildly. As Robin Marlar had prophetically put it, the cricket authorities were, 'not geared up to withstand this kind of business piracy'.

In Pakistan and the West Indies crises broke out involving the signed WSC players and their local authorities – players were selected to play for their countries, then un-selected by the opposing Establishment forces. It turned out the rioting at Sabina Park against Bobby Simpson's team, sparked by an umpiring decision, was mostly aimed by the people against the WICBC. WSC players had been banned from the Tests by the board, seen as white and reactionary and described as being of the 'autocratic, oligarchic planter class'.

In England, Kent advised that it would not be re-signing its four WSC players Asif Iqbal, Alan Knott, Derek Underwood and Bob Woolmer after 1978. The Kent board split viciously over the decision and former Kent hero and wicketkeeper for England Les Ames described the action as 'repugnant and distasteful'. The ICC was in stasis, the TCCB shooting blindly. Sussex announced it was not re-engaging WSC fast bowler John Snow, then blasted away at Tony Greig, sacking him as captain of Sussex and banning him from playing for two months for writing a newspaper article critical of Geoffrey Boycott. 'Boycott has the uncanny knack of being where the fast bowlers aren't,' Greig wrote in defending WSC players against Boycott's criticisms.

At this point in the drama there was no more high-falutin talk of the philosophy of cricket or the elegant traditions of the great game or any more morally princi-pled positions being taken by anyone, particularly in the Establishment. The dispute had gone beyond nebulous moral and ethical attack or defence, it was now bitter, practical, personal, internally divisive. National boards managed to hold firm in their official announcements, but there was known to be conflict, unpleasantness and confusion behind closed doors. Cricket was eating its own entrails.

4
RESOLUTION

WSC's second season, the Australian summer of 1978–79, was months away and with the administrators and executives busy organising the future and fighting the war, preparing the stage, the cricketers found themselves again like actors in the wings waiting to go on. It was going to be quite a wait – though some of the World and West Indies cricketers were still playing in various forums, the first WSC matches were not due to start until late October and the Australians had a whole eight months of no pressure – a dangerous position. Elite sportsmen can never fully relax over their off-season, they can't let fitness, reaction times and focus drift too far or it becomes almost impossible to get them back. They lose their edge.

The teams always had Kerry on their backs, growling at them about training, doing his best to set proper schedules and agendas for their training regimen. He was paying them good fucking money – no one was going to get 'fat and lazy' on his chequebook.

The term is relative in the rarefied world of the elite sportsperson. Australia's legendary darling of the 2000 Olympics, Cathy Freeman, was once described to the press as 'fat' by her ex-trainer. At the time she was, of course, lean as a leopard. The reporters got into a lather trying to get photos of Cathy looking like Aretha Franklin, but they got it wrong. They didn't quite get that 'fat', to a world-class athlete, simply means slightly out of condition, not up to absolute and optimum fitness. Same with 'lazy', which means not deep in the zone or fully focused.

Champion sportspeople work on different criteria than the rest of us, they are just gifted – the ones who lined up twice when physical abilities were being dished out. Like virtuoso musicians who, after spending half an hour with an instrument they have never seen, can produce music it takes twenty years to learn, elite athletes can not only master but excel in any sport they choose. At school they lead the cricket, the football, the swimming, the tennis. They then leave school and take up golf, blitzing the courses, vaguely wondering if they might make this their high-paying career. Try playing them at snooker, or even pool in a pub. Their personal goals are higher, their personal abilities are supreme, their focus is supernatural, their will to win obsessive. Elite sports men and women are how F. Scott Fitzgerald described the rich – they're different from you and me. By their criterion fat and lazy is how the rest of us are all the time – probably exactly how they see us.

While the World and West Indies players made their own arrangements, Ian Chappell, urged on by Kerry, did his best to drill his Australians into lean machines. Chappell never had any troubles with training, by his own admission he could enjoy a long, wet lunch with 'six or seven beers', then go home, put on shorts and a T-shirt and do quarter-hour sprints.

But…'Training did not come naturally to Australian cricketers,' wrote Gideon Haigh, 'Some smoked, all drank and few ran when they could walk'. Hauling big men like Gary Gilmour or naturally phlegmatic characters like Doug Walters across the line was never going to be easy. These two champions had their own views on fitness and cricketing ability, but it didn't accord with Kerry's or Chappell's. Still, they were targeted along with everyone else.

To motivate his players, Kerry used the whip he knew most about – money. As well as being expected to do the usual work at the nets, bowling and batting, plus catching and athletic work round the field to test their overall condition, the cricketers were given set distances to run in a set amount of time, a minimum of 2500 metres – 2.5 kilometres – in 15 minutes, or else

Kerry would knock an amount of money off their contracts. The players even suspected the Boss sent spies to check up on them. Strange, anonymous members of the CPH family would suddenly appear, eagle-eyed at training, watching closely, then disappear without explaining their presence.

Twenty-two of the 24 Australian players relished the whole running program. Mick Malone is reputed to have gone well over 4 kilometres in the given time and most of the others were close to that, well over 3 kilometres at least.

'But the two problems were Gus Gilmour and Dougy [Walters], and they both took the attitude, "Fuck it",' says Ian Chappell. Both men were playing fine enough cricket, both swashbuckling batsmen, handy bowlers (in the One Day International Inaugural World Cup two years earlier Gilmour took 6–14), and despite their abhorrence of fitness training, outstanding fieldsmen. Gilmour had taken to limited-over cricket as if it had been invented for him and Walters' laid back demeanor, his legendary unorthodox batting and 'when you least expect it' bowling had made him not only the most popular Australian cricketer of the time (and possibly ever), but a secret weapon who had a knack of scoring centuries and taking wickets just when things were looking blackest.

Both men, like their peers, were true athletes, it was just something stubborn in their make-up that made them decide training was bullshit. 'They got pretty stubborn about it,' says Chappell, 'and neither of these two guys were the sort of guys who were going to relent – particularly Doug'. After cajoling and protests and threats, Walters finally put down his can of beer and his cigarette, took to the track and ran 2501 metres in the 15 minutes. A metre more than he had to as an 'up you' bonus for Kerry.

With the beginnings of a leg injury that would dog the rest of his career – caused by his bulky frame on legs that weren't made for it – Gilmour was holding out and Kerry was making angry noises about fining him a fortune or even ripping up his contract. One night, Ian Chappell, Gilmour, Austin Robertson and the team manager Geoff Forsaith were drinking in the Sheraton Hotel in Perth where they were staying and the subject of Kerry's threats came up. 'Gus was a pretty useful cricketer, we didn't need him out of the team,' says Chappell, 'so I said Gus for fuck's sake will you go for a run. And run as far as you can. If you have to cheat, cheat, but come back and tell me you've done it'.

There was a park down the hill from the Sheraton a lot further than 2500 metres round, so that was to be the distance. While the others kept drinking Gilmour took off, came back a little later, puffing, and said, 'Yeah, I've done it'.

Robertson, the guy who had to front Kerry, wasn't convinced. Kerry would need an official time and distance. But no one had a stopwatch and no one felt like traipsing down to the park to watch Gilmour disappear off into the dark. The debate and the beers continued late into the night till at about 11 o'clock they hit on a neat solution. They piled into Forsaith's BMW and, headlights illuminating Gilmour's way, keeping a weather eye out for cops, drove around the park beside him, timing him, watching the car's odometer the whole way. 'We made sure we went 2550 metres,' said Chappell, 'I said righto, now you can tell Kerry we've measured it and it's official'. Gilmour was safe.

The intensity of the fitness regimen was another WSC innovation. Before WSC, cricketers had a degree of physical condition tuned to the game of the day. After WSC spectators never again saw the blimpy batsmen who relied on technique and timing at the crease lumbering down to complete their single, or their two. They no longer saw fieldsmen trotting off in the direction of a ball rolling happily towards the pickets. Thanks to fitness the game came down to one of more exquisite timing. Cricket point-scoring was calibrated to finer and finer degrees, with athletic batsmen dashing and diving to grab a sneaky single, fielders doing their lying-down hip-skid along the grass to bring a sure four to a three, fielders taking catches their fathers and grandfathers would have *known* to be impossible. The tough conditioning gladdened the heart of WSC's proud new supremo, Andrew Caro. 'The Australians became the fittest side in the competition, and possibly the fittest team ever to play first class cricket in Australia,' he wrote.

★

The hot Australian summer of 1978–79 was one of those unforgettable seasons when change and excitement were in the air. The 1970s were on the fade – what will the 1980s be like? There was a clue in Margaret Thatcher and Ronald Reagan, just appearing over the rise. A new Pope, Karol Wojtyla from Poland, the youngest Pope of the twentieth century, was elected, self-styled 'Wild One' rocker Johnny O'Keefe died in Sydney, and over the Bass Strait a young pilot, Frederick Valentich, disappeared in his light plane a short time after radioing that a long UFO with green lights was hovering round his Cessna. Cricket was everywhere, the Australian public blitzed with radio and TV ads from both sides, Channel 9 coming out with an impressive hour-long documentary *The WSC Story* produced by David Hill, a slick piece of propaganda that made the 'new' cricket look like something from the future and WSC look not only legitimate but cool.

And it was in brilliant colour. Colour TV was introduced into Australia in 1975 and Australians went for it in swarms – one of the world's fastest uptakes. When the 1978–79 summer arrived nearly two-thirds of Australian households had made the big switch. Nothing was black and white anymore.

With the start of the hot weather, the Establishment and WSC began hurling its thunderbolt cricket matches at each other. Australia's six Ashes Tests against Mike Brearley's England team, were now led by a keen young batsman named Graham Yallop – the old gunfighter Bobby Simpson, having stepped in to do his job, had gone back to the farm to enjoy the twilight years. These Ashes matches were up against WSC's five Supertests. The historic state-versus-state Sheffield Shield continued but WSC had its Country Cup series dubbed 'Packer's Sheffield Shield'. Late in the season Pakistan arrived to play two test matches against Yallop's team, but WSC was still hauling in crowds to its limited-over games.

Hype and publicity. The noise of battle filled the airwaves. But in this contest, at least, the young turks of WSC were punching below their weight. Andrew

Caro had noted early that the WSC audience would increasingly be one that preferred the Bee Gees over ABC concerts. The pop charts had the Village People singing *YMCA*, Queen with *Fat Bottomed Girls*, Dire Straits' *Sultans of Swing,* and now that the old rockstar Johnny O'Keefe was dead, iconoclastic bad boys Cold Chisel buried the past, sticking it to pop tradition by coming out with *You're Thirteen, You're Beautiful, and You're Mine*, featuring splashes of female nudity all over the album cover. The other song of the season, top of the pops, was *C'mon Aussie, C'mon*, the WSC anthem.

Earlier in the year Kerry and a few of his top insiders had kicked around how to sell the coming season to the punters. The vision of mums and dads and kids frolicking at half time on the beautifully lit VFL Park, inspired by Cornell witnessing just that during matches in New Zealand, was the template for an advertising campaign aimed at the family. This is not dad and his ocker mates on the SCG Hill getting pissed and sledging batsmen. 'You couldn't hit the water if you fell out of a bloody boat!' WSC cricket was to be like baseball in the United States – come to the family party and enjoy the sporting spectacular. But it was finally decided this was not the way to go. Scrap that. Kerry and John Cornell, in particular, wanted the WSC public to be cheering for Australia, for the nation as they always had.

It was another astute insight. Patriotism, apart from all the warm sense of tradition it brought, would help brand WSC as something other than mercenary cricket and would help blur the distinction between WSC cricket and the Establishment matches. The more WSC imprinted as the dreaded 'exhibition matches' in the minds of the public, the less chance it had of maximising its cultural impact. And there was another imperative – to put the Australian (and World) cricketers back on the pedestal they once occupied. As Max Walker had pointed out a year earlier, the guys had been famously playing to immense crowds, packed stadiums, hundreds of thousands of people. Now, despite the best efforts of the WSC machine, they were walking out to do battle before audiences a tenth of the size they were used to. Many of the WSC cricketers experienced being called un-Australian or worse, traitors, by people in the street or at airports. The cricketers knew, deep down, they weren't playing for Australia anymore.

They didn't articulate this, but they felt it. John Cornell says he could 'see the looks on their faces'.

WSC needed a theme, an anthem, a war cry, a call to arms, something to put the old pride and spring back into the players' step and something to convince the punters that these guys were playing for fucking Straya.

As Paul Hogan's agent, Cornell had dealings with

two young creatives in the ad agency Hertz Walpole, Alan Morris and Allan Johnston, who had launched Winfield cigarettes using Hogan as front man. The pair had teamed up a few years earlier as employees at Hertz Walpole, creating the timeless jingle for Meadow Lea margarine, 'You oughta be congratulated', and were about to take the leap into creating MOJO, the hottest advertising agency in 1980s Australia. Any ad campaign these two were involved in meant an immediate and spectacular climb in sales, particularly if they had written a theme song to go with it. These themes, sung by Allan Johnston in his appealing and distinctive gravel Aussie tones, had people humming advertising slogans in the street – a marketers' dream.

'I said to Kerry I've got a mate I'm going to see about a song,' says Cornell, 'Named Big Al'. 'Big Al?' he said, 'sounds like a criminal'.

I said, 'No mate, different sort of mafia'.

Big Al (the tag is ironic) Johnston and his mate Allan Morris were perfect examples of a particular mafia, that rarified group of advertising's high creatives in the lamented lost world of the balmy long-lunch seventies. Johnston describes how he and his mate Morris operated. 'We used to get in early at 7 o'clock in the morning,' he says, 'and drink coffee and smoke cigarettes until about 11 or 12. And if we didn't have something by then we'd go to lunch for about 4 hours. Then come back and try again and usually we'd get nothing – we'd be writing nonsense'. They often continued for weeks like this, struggling to come up with a decent melody and lyric for a jingle.

It was different though, when Cornell 'just dropped in' out of nowhere one afternoon and explained the brief, 'to try and make the players feel better about what they were doing and to get people to come to the cricket'. Easy – let's give that a shot. With Cornell watching, smiling his enigmatic smile, the two Als started fiddling with a guitar and some offhand lyrics. 'Lillee's pounding down like a machine, Pascoe's making divots in the green.' It rhymes! 'It really flowed pretty quickly,' says Johnston, 'one of the quickest jobs we'd ever done'.

With the juices flowing, that same afternoon after Cornell departed they grabbed an old four-track TEAC tape recorder and with a couple of guys from the office singing chorus and Johnston on the guitar they put down a rough demo.

The chorus was: 'Come on Australia, let's show them what we're made of. Come on Australia, come on'. It also rhymes! As long as you sing it right, says Johnston, 'Come on Austraya. Let's show 'em what we're mayda…'

Serendipitously, and fortunately for pop and cricket history, the court cases banning WSC from using the word 'Australia' to describe their team meant this first shot at the anthem was stillborn. The two Als kept their main lyrics, expanding on them and using, strangely enough, the a, a, b, b, a, rhyming form, the complex anapaestic foot of the centuries-old limerick.

> *Lillee's pounding down like a machine,*
> *Pascoe's making divots in the green,*
> *Marshy's taking wickets,*
> *Hooksey's clearing pickets,*
> *And the Chappell's eyes have got that killer gleam.*

Then came the clincher. Okay, so we can't use 'Australia', but we can go one better. The chorus became, 'Come on Aussie come on, come on. Come on Aussie come on' – immediately iconic and still one of the unforgettable lyrics of Australian pop music. Its adaptability was quickly recognised and soon there was a Reggae version with its characteristic accent on the off beat, sung by the West Indians. This time the chorus, instead of being a supportive chant, became a taunt – images showing West Indian batsmen at the crease giving a beckoning signal, 'come onnn'. Twenty-six years after it was first penned, *C'mon Aussie* was a hit for pop star Shannon Noll with new, up-to-date lyrics. And as long as new names are added to the Australian cricket team's board of honour, the anthem is endlessly adaptable to fresh rhymes.

Cornell took the demo to Kerry and a few of the WSC top echelon, who immediately recognised the anthem's power. By this time the two Als had polished and enriched their lyrics and the form of the song, opening it with Johnston's unmistakeable voice delivering a low, spoken preamble that gave a nod to Ian Chappell's fitness campaign.

> *You've been training all the winter,*
> *And there's not a team that's fitter,*
> *And that's the way it's gotta be.*
> *'Cause you're up against the best you know,*
> *This is Supertest you know,*
> *And you've gotta beat the best the world has seen...*

Shortly afterwards the song was put down in its final sophisticated form, credited to 'The Mojo Singers', among them one John 'Strop' Cornell. 'John was in the chorus,' Johnston laughs, 'You hear him scream out in the original recording. In the middle of the choruses, in between one of the breaks, between one 'come on' and another, you hear him go, 'Come on!' That's him'. On 10 January 1979, *C'mon Aussie, C'mon* hit the Number One spot on the Australian pop charts.

With their anthem building on the airwaves from early November 1978, WSC scheduled for its cricketers a punishing summer of five Supertests played over four days each by the Australian, West Indies and World stars, an International Cup series of 27 matches under lights in Melbourne and Sydney, and the Country Cup, a four-sided contest between Australia, West Indies, World and 'Cavaliers' – the Cavaliers being those undeserving and unhappy players left over after the top sides had been chosen. WSC played a total of 88 days' cricket that summer, an awful lot in a period of four months.

The relative success of the world's first day–night games at VFL Park the previous season meant the WSC insiders were optimistic of their chances of a decent crowd when the huge SCG lighting towers – dubbed 'Packer's cigars' by the public – were turned on. But no one was quite prepared for what happened.

On the night of 28 November, 50,000 people filled the SCG to watch the Australians play the West Indies. When the gates opened in the early afternoon, 5000 people – an acceptable WSC total just a year earlier – were waiting to get in. As the afternoon waned and the cricket hotted up another 25,000 arrived. The dream was coming true. Kids, still in their school uniforms, began pouring in after 3.30 in the afternoon. Then more and more people turned up, mums picked up kids from school and dads from work then drove to the SCG with the hamper in the car boot. Young women and men left work, met up to drink in Paddington pubs, then went on to party at the cricket. And still they came.

Exactly one year and four days earlier Kerry and John Cornell, full of nervous anticipation, had spied with their binoculars out the back of the VFL Park grandstand a few isolated cars rolling into the massive carpark looking lost and hesitant. They saw a huge bus or two, disgorging three or four lost people. Now, as the sun went down in the background, they looked out to the western side of Sydney's great cricket oval and saw a riot of 10,000 women and men gathered in a huge conga line, pressing forward anxiously to be allowed to be part of the spectacle. Kerry, urged on by police getting decidedly nervous at the turbulence, ordered the gates to be thrown open. Let 'em in for free. The people poured in. Members of the SCG, overwhelmingly male, overwhelmingly on the side of the Establishment, stayed clear of the game so Kerry ordered the Members Stand doors opened, and for the first time in history women were welcomed to the SCG's inner sanctum.

On the field the gods of the game, still in traditional whites, were doing battle. The crowd, partisan, beefed up, loving every minute of it, did its best to take the roof off when Dennis Lillee got Viv Richards with his third ball. They roared approval, they screamed 'Come on Aussie!' to the grinning players, they sang the anthem and they knew the words.

Up in the crowded stands the whole WSC family was gathered to witness their triumph, including avuncular Harry Chester, beaming pride at what his boy had achieved. Cornell, Delvene, Robertson and Hogan saw it all and remembered the warm afternoons in Neutral Bay when the vague idea came up of maybe putting on 'some games at the end of the year or something'. Instead, Kerry Packer, the essence of the WSC imagination, had gone off on a journey of his own, finally bringing them and 50,000 other souls home to this place and time.

Cornell says he was particularly chuffed that the crowd was singing along with such a happy familiarity with the words to the song. They had, of course, learned the lyrics from the WSC airwave blitz of the previous three weeks.

To him it was all about the public's attention span. 'I wanted to hold it till there was about three weeks to go,' he says, 'then saturate the airwaves all at once. Any longer than that and they forget about it by the time you're on. We did the same thing with *Croc Dundee*. Just a bit less than three weeks and you can get 'em – they can plan what they're going to do with their time.'

In the three weeks leading up to that radiant SCG night Cornell had been clandestinely going in to Channel 9 in Sydney to talk with the on-air program controller, purportedly on Kerry's behalf. 'I've just come from Kerry – which I hadn't – how many times have you got *C'mon Aussie* on tonight?' He would check the program controller's advertising schedule, noting how many times the ads were being aired, and feign horror – 'Kerry wants more than *that*. He wants you to drop this ad, drop that ad, and put the cricket anthem on instead'.

Standing beside a beaming Kerry that night, listening to the anthem being sung in lusty 50,000-part harmony, Cornell decided it was time to fess up. Unsure what Kerry's reaction was going to be he said, 'I think this is probably a good time to tell you, Kerry, I confess. I've been going in to Channel 9 and getting them to put the *C'mon Aussie* ads on and dropping other stuff'. Kerry gazed down at him and said, 'Good onya son'.

At half-time Tony Greig arrived with fellow World players Bob Woolmer, Dennis Amiss and their wives. They'd been playing in Orange in Central Western New South Wales and were picked up by Kerry's chopper. 'It was a very emotional night,' he says, admitting that when he walked in and witnessed the extraordinary spectacle he found himself close to tears. 'All the hard work had been worth it,' he said, 'WSC had been accepted'.

When the game, appropriately won by the Australians, ended at 9.20 pm, the crowd drifted off home and the summer evening cooled. The lights were still on, shining promise and good fortune on the whole WSC enterprise when Greig found Kerry, a lone figure high in the stands, gazing out over the empty green of the oval, thinking his thoughts and dreaming his dreams.

'This is it,' Greig said.

'Yes,' said Kerry, 'I think you're right'.

That historic night was the beginning of the endgame. With WSC powering along, especially after that massive success, Kerry and the ACB now began carefully dancing round each other. Parish and Steele had witnessed the triumphant evening and, knowing it was too big to ignore, had put out a communiqué commending WSC on its success and its 'excellent' crowd – the French government commending the English government on its 'excellent' result at Waterloo. The year 1979 arrived with the feeling that this could go on no longer.

Kerry saw this shift towards rapprochement as a fine opportunity to gouge an advantage from the old enemy. He made it a condition of talks that the ACB make Jeff

Thomson, the fastest bowler in the world, available to him.

The loss of Jeff Thomson the previous year, with all its high emotion, still burned for Kerry, a man who never, ever, forgot or could easily put anything aside. When Thomson signed with WSC then reneged, going back in chaotic circumstances to traditional cricket, he had infuriated Kerry who had to be talked out of chasing him through the courts. No Thommo meant that WSC missed out on the spectacular Hollywood pairing of Lillee and Thomson (dubbed 'Lilian Thomson'). These two champions bowling from opposite ends made for terrifying cricket and fast-spinning turnstiles – they were a promoter's dream, the Redford and Newman of international cricket.

Last season Thomson had played for the Australian cricket team under Bobby Simpson and had even been Simpson's vice-captain for the West Indies tour, but now he was reported as being not happy at all, either with Simpson or the quality of play. He and Simpson had not got on well and Thomson declared he wouldn't play under Simpson again. Simpson had retired but it didn't improve Thomson's mood. Rumours of his impending decision to follow Simpson into retirement had swirled about cricket circles during the winter of 1978, but here it was spring and he was not only still playing but contracted to the ACB to bowl for Australia in the forth-coming Ashes series.

He didn't want to. He wanted back into WSC. Asked why by the press he said, 'I want to play with my mates. And with blokes who can catch'.

But the ACB had his feet nailed to the floor. Sure, Simpson had been allowed to retire, he was just going off into the twilight, but they decided their star fast bowler was bloody well going nowhere. They knew if Thomson, who apparently had a few financial problems, was allowed to 'retire' from Establishment cricket he'd immediately sign up with you-know-who. Meanwhile Kerry, watching all this closely, still keenly wanted him and let his operatives know that if there was any chance at all, the demon bowler should be re-signed to WSC.

When a change of ownership at Thomson's Bris-bane radio station 4IP altered the legal landscape, they decided to give it a shot. A WSC contract was drawn up for Thomson and it was arranged that he would retire from ACB cricket. Having decided he'd had enough of cricket he'd officially tell the ACB he was retiring, then – who would have thought – shortly later find himself back amongst his mates at WSC. The ACB, smelling a rat, immediately replied with their own letter saying, 'see you in court, Jeff'.

In the NSW Equity Court, Thomson was put

through the grinder by a vindictive ACB. As their counsel pounded into him, Thomson sat in court conspicuously reading fishing magazines. But when it came down to it, what was the ACB going to do? Shove him into a car, drive him to the venue, make him put on white clothing and put a ball in his hand? If he didn't want to play cricket there was no way on earth they could force him.

The ACB's point of view was bloody-minded but it was one they saw as legitimate – again they were operating on justified high dudgeon. They knew what the slippery characters in WSC were up to and they decided, yet again, not to let them ride roughshod, or at least to make it as hard for them as possible. And they were right. WSC was doing nothing more or less than deceitful poaching, an art they had polished to perfection over the past 18 months.

Thomson struggled under cross-examination, a hapless witness, and the court case was a farce. As Andrew Caro put it, 'Thomson appeared simple, World Series Cricket appeared bullying, and the Australian Board were vindictive'. This spiteful case was the last of the head-to-head clashes World Series Cricket was to have with the ACB. Unsurprisingly the court declared Thomson's new WSC contract, its ink still wet, completely null and void. He was allowed to 'retire', of course, who could stop him? But he wasn't allowed to sign again with WSC until 31 March 1979, effectively banning him from cricket for the rest of the 1978–79 season.

This was a problem not to be countenanced. Kerry had a major WSC tour of the West Indies coming up – five Supertests plus a series of one-dayers – starting on 20 February and now he had a sniff of Thomson he wasn't going to let his prize get away. Kerry, negotiator extraordinaire, smoothly informed the ACB that if the two sides were to move towards détente there would be no real progress unless the board could demonstrate its bona fides by, say… agreeing to free Thomson up for the West Indies tour.

They bought it. So for the third time, a contract was written up for Thomson to be brought into the WSC fold and just a few days before the team was to leave Australia, Austin Robertson and Ian Chappell, hot new contract in hand, went off to his home in Bankstown to get him to sign up. Strangely, Thomson wasn't there. They hung around for an hour or so having tea with Thommo's parents, but there was no appearance from Jeff.

A few days later at a final meeting in Kerry's office Kerry was in a high and happy mood. This West Indies tour would be a smash. The Windies might have a brace of fast bowlers, but we've got Lillee, Pascoe, Thomson…

He stopped. 'Thommo signed, didn't he,' he said,

looking at Ian Chappell.

Chappell assured him that, well, on the first attempt there were cups of tea with Mum and Dad but for some reason Thommo didn't turn up. But since then Austin's been onto it and it's now all fixed. Kerry, mood coming down, swung on Austin Robertson. 'Has Thomson signed?'

'Well, apparently he wasn't at the house because his lawyer told him not to be there, but we've since spoken to the solicitor and Lynton tells me it's all fixed'.

Kerry, now glaring, the temperature in the room plummeting, swung on Lynton Taylor. 'Has fuckin' Thomson signed?'

'No problem,' said Taylor calmly, 'I've spoken to his solicitors and it's all in order. Our legal guys've got it all fixed'.

With Chappell and Robertson choking in the background, the single unfortunate WSC lawyer in the room braced himself. Kerry pointed the mean finger. 'It's a fucking simple question. Has he put fucking pen to fucking paper?!'

'Not exactly,' said the lawyer, 'but it's not a problem. I've spoken to Jim Thynne at Allen Allen & Hemsley and he's got it all sorted'.

'Where,' said Kerry in a very low voice, 'the *fuck* is Thynne?'

At that moment lawyer Jim Thynne was unfortunately holidaying up on the Gold Coast. 'Right,' says Kerry, 'I'll fuck that holiday up right now.' He smashed his hand down on an intercom button and ordered his secretary to find a relaxed and unwinding Thynne who was dragged to the phone to be hit by a white-hot blast. Thomson was signed at the last possible minute before he jumped on a plane to the Caribbean with his mates who could catch.

★

The WSC Australians' tour of the West Indies from February to April 1979 was never going to be a cakewalk, the schedule packed so tightly there was very little down time for anyone. Past tours had featured four or five tests, a few casual four-day games and a couple of one-dayers. Plenty of time to lounge round the pool and enjoy the glorious weather, the rum and the hospitality, and more importantly recharge the batteries. But Ian Chappell's men were faced with five, five-day Supertests and twelve one-day matches – all up 37 full days of cricket between 23 February and 13 April. The continual-travel itinerary and the gruelling cricket schedule pushed the cricketers to the very edge of what they were capable of, mentally and physically. Added to that, the polarisation between the Establishment and WSC meant there were darkly simmering political undercurrents as a backdrop to the tour. The West Indies crowds, volatile at the calmest of times, were particularly unpredictable that season. The previous May they had rioted in Jamaica against Bobby Simpson's XI, the Australian team dashing off Sabina Park in Jamaica with bottles and rocks raining down on them.

After being blasted off the field in four days in the first Supertest at Sabina Park, Ian Chappell's Australians managed to claw back a draw in the second Supertest in Barbados, then pulled out a win in the third at Queens Park in Trinidad.

But only just. When the Australians ran out local hero Deryck Murray in the second innings rocks and bottles began peppering the field. The runout was close, excruciatingly close, and the crowd thought Murray had been given a bad call. More bottles, more catcalling and whistling, more commotion in the crowd – typical early signs of a full-scale, game-ending riot. Remembering last season in Jamaica, the umpires began, as Ian Chappell later put it, 'getting twitchy'. At Chappell's urging Murray got to the ground PA microphone and told the crowd he was convinced the umpire's runout decision was correct – he was definitely out. It worked, they settled. But it was a close call.

The next match at the Bourda Ground in Guyana, the fourth Supertest, found a place in cricket history. It didn't bring the tour crashing down but it was a climax of sorts, for the cricketers and for WSC itself. The truncated game was miraculously played, but, as the match report states: 'No play on first and second day due to rain and riot'.

The players woke up on day one to find it had been pouring rain overnight and was still raining. The day's play was cancelled even before anyone left for the ground. Day two was bright and sunny, the pitch, which had been covered, was fine, but Chappell and West Indies captain Clive Lloyd decided the boggy outfield was too dangerous to play on.

Here was a major problem. Although the Bourda staff had been told play might not go ahead and not to let ticketholders onto the ground, the gates had been opened at dawn. By the time Lloyd and Chappell decided against playing, the ground was packed. All through the long hot morning as the day heated up 13,000 spectators milled about drinking rum and waiting for something to happen. By lunchtime a feisty, nasty mood was sweeping the ground. In the early afternoon the first few bottles were thrown, the odd rock or two, timber from the stands. Knowing that to cancel play altogether would bring the whole place crashing down, the captains and umpires, team managers and ground officials agreed that some kind game had to happen out there. They'd start the match a little before four in the afternoon and give the crowd at least some cricket. A West Indian announcer then infuriated Ian Chappell by putting it out on the ground PA that play would start at 2.40 pm.

When nothing happened at the appointed time, the crowd, which by now had been lowering rum in the blazing heat for about seven hours, went off its collective head, trampling the security fences, hurling bits of metal, chairs, timber, rocks and bottles, and heading for the pavilion. Both teams ducked into their respective dressing rooms, shoved heavy tables against the doors and prepared for battle. In the West Indies dressing room Joel Garner said it felt, 'a bit like I imagine Americans felt at the Alamo'. In the Australian dressing room, as bricks and timber crashed through the windows, the players put on helmets, visors pulled down to protect their eyes from flying glass, grabbed bats as weapons and prepared to repel all comers. The Australians' armed security guard had bolted into their dressing room with them.

'This security guard had a pistol,' says Ian Chappell, 'so I went and stood right next to him. I said, "Mate you've got the gun, I'm with you". We all stood there for a few minutes, and the next thing we hear shots outside'.

'I said to the security bloke, "Oh we're right now, the riot police are here". He said, "No man, that's not the riot police – that's their side". I thought, "Oh fuck, this is not good".'

It was nearly an hour before peace was restored. The riot squad did turn up and with baton charges swept the crowd back and out the gates. Ground authorities discovered later that someone had tried to set fire to the wooden pavilion, but luckily it didn't take. The Australians got the message that two of the West Indies players had been cut by flying glass, so they grabbed bottles of Heineken beer and went off to the opposition dressing room 'for a beer or two and a chat'. Chappell says he spoke with Deryck Murray whose explanation for the mayhem was the populace's high discontent with graft and corruption amongst the country's leadership and the fact that the whole of Guyana was unnerved by the infamous 'Jonestown Massacre' in the north of the country, only two months earlier when 912 members of a US religious sect had committed suicide – the largest mass self-killing in modern history.

Later that night Chappell and Rodney Marsh were dining in their hotel when they were approached by a young West Indian man who recognised them and wanted to buy them a drink. As the three chatted the young guy mentioned he had been at the Bourda Ground that day, rioting, throwing bottles. When they asked him why he had replied, 'I just got caught up in the moment'.

The following day the ground was cleaned up and play began. It was, understandably, a draw, and so was the final exhausting, draining fifth Supertest in Antigua.

★

Meanwhile, as his battle-weary cricketers bled for him, Kerry's more accommodating relationship with the ACB was gathering steam. A new dynamic had entered the WSC equation – it was becoming increasingly clear the war wasn't made for the long term. As Imran Khan later wrote, 'For all the excitement of WSC I really missed the tension and commitment of real Test cricket. Had WSC gone for another season, as originally planned, I think a number of players, including me, would have dropped out'.

Thirty is considered a watershed age for elite cricketers who, like most sportspeople, tend to perform at their peak through their twenties. After that it comes down to a season by season, game by game, proposition. They last as long as they can, until injury or poor form or

both, kill them off. By 1979, a lot of Kerry's key cricketers were senior stars and they would, in another season
or so, be veterans. Gideon Haigh quotes the statistics:
'Ten of twenty-three Australians, five of eighteen West
Indians and no fewer than fourteen of nineteen World
players were past thirty'. If this thing was going to go
much longer WSC would be on a continual treadmill of
recruiting, poaching, confrontation.

Other factors were clearly at play. Kerry, the ACB
and the ICC knew it was negotiating time. The ACB
spent that summer unhappily watching Mike Brearley's
visiting England team thrash the Australian XI. Six tests
were played and England won five of them. Worse, England won three of the first four, so crowds didn't bother
turning up for the final two dead games. For the ACB
the season was the writing on the wall. Something had
to be done.

In January, a three-man ICC delegation arrived in
Australia and immediately went into a huddle with the
ACB in Melbourne. Word filtered out that they were
working on a peace plan, after all what the hell else
would they be talking about? Then reporters stumbled
on a Sydney meeting between the ICC trio and Kerry,
Andrew Caro, Lynton Taylor and Harry Chester. Clearly
some kind of peace was in the offing. The journalists and
cricket commentators began writing anew of the war,

examining the battles of the past two years and commenting on an end to hostilities.

But Kerry was ignoring the war. It's just business – chaotic, strange and debilitating business to be sure, but business just the same. His focus remained where it had always been, on the *reasons* for the war. The three English administrators copped a blast. 'I can't understand why I've got members of the MCC in my office discussing what is basically an Australian problem,' he's quoted as telling them. 'If I'm going to speak to anyone, I want to speak to Parish and Steele.' The English delegation got the message loud and clear. They authorised Parish and Steele to negotiate with Kerry (but only Kerry) on their behalf and high-tailed it back to London. Charged with this carte blanche brief, Bob Parish, even though he had some misgivings, knew that he and Ray Steele were the ones to bring this whole thing to an end. From here on it was just a matter of detail.

What was it that changed the mood in the opening weeks of 1979? Exhaustion – possibly. A wish to get back to the game's civilised norms – probably. But mostly it was because a special moment was looming – the ABC's rights to televise Establishment cricket were due to expire at the end of March. Both sides had known all along that this critical moment would come. It had seemed so far off for so long, now here it was almost upon them and the ACB knew it was their moment of truth. Kerry's scorched earth blitzkrieg reaction to being knocked back for exclusive TV rights in June 1976 had bruised and battered the whole corpus of cricket. If he was refused again, what the hell was he capable of? Kerry and Bob Parish met in Sydney in mid February 1979 for a few preliminary words on how to go about sorting things out.

When he got word of this meeting General Manager of the ABC, Talbot Duckmanton, would have experienced a sudden and terrible feeling in the pit of his stomach. And it would have kept him up nights when, a week later, the ACB's Ray Steele met with Kerry, Lynton Taylor and Harry Chester. At this meeting Kerry slung in his original bid of half a million dollars per year, again easily topping the ABC's $200,000. Duckmanton was witnessing 23 years of the ACB/ABC love affair coming to a crashing close and, given the shenanigans he'd witnessed since 1976, there was not a damn thing he could do about it. He tut-tutted and memoed and made frantic phonecalls, but knew he was a dead man, forced to work at the margin, finally made an irrelevancy as the big guys carved up what he and his organisation had considered their birthright for more than a generation. It had taken Kerry three years and four times that in millions of dollars to make himself an inevitability. He had lost a little skin, but not as much as his opponents who right now just wanted it all to end.

★

Kerry might have had as much battle fatigue as his weary cricketers, but his injuries, if they existed at all, were internal and easily overcome. His shock-troop gladiators though, were having a hard time of it. Pushed to their limits they were breaking down to an unprecedented degree. Injuries are an integral part of all sport – there are almost as many injuries carried by teenage girl gymnasts as there are by 30-year-old Rugby warhorses. Hookes and McCosker's jaws, Lillee's ankle, a smashed finger for Ian Chappell and many others, a sore shoulder here, a torn muscle there, the odd sprain, are par for the course, injuries like these come with the territory. But exhaustion and stress can change the matrix, and Kerry's players were close to collapse.

Players always reach that point in the long game when they can see the end coming up to meet them and they know they need to dig into that part of them they keep in reserve till this moment. At such times, they will tell you, pain and bodily stress don't count for much – they've already gone through the pain barrier. Elite sports men and women are used to hurt – the very best learn to operate well through physical trauma – it's a characteristic of champions that they continue to excel while carrying wreckage that would sideline mortal players. But in the high-emotion endgame they are particularly prone to injury, badly, unexpectedly, and sometimes in a way that brings an end to a career.

Things inexplicably go wrong. Luck changes. In Trinidad for the third Supertest, Kerry O'Keefe, running to keep fit, was hit by a car, his medial ligaments were torn away and his leg smashed in three places.

Lillee's continual back and ankle niggles continued, but – champion – he pushed through them. Then January 1979, a thigh injury caught him, adding to the hamstring difficulties he had already been nursing. Wayne Daniel, Michael Holding, Joel Garner and Roy Fredericks carried increasingly worsening injuries into the final matches. Rick McCosker badly damaged his thumb. Thomson, cleared to play but not fully match-fit, experienced painful back and leg spasms. One of the clearest examples was West Indies wicketkeeper Deryck Murray who that 1978–79 season suffered a dislocated shoulder. He had played top cricket without a major injury for 15 years. Greg Chappell, also blessedly free of major injury, strained his back. Gary Gilmour pulled a hamstring. Rodney Marsh was close to exhaustion. Ian

Chappell, now 35, developed a painful spur in his right heel.

Batsman Ian Davis didn't go on the tour, citing family pressures, perhaps having some insight into what the others were facing. 'I used to eat, sleep, shower and shit cricket,' Haigh quotes him as saying. 'But when I got married I did realise that there was more in life than cricket, and that there was no point dying for it.'

Pressure at that strange time fell overwhelmingly on the shoulders of Ian Chappell. Journalist Phil Wilkins, the only Australian journalist covering the West Indies tour, wrote, 'No one has ever known the pressure Ian was under on that tour. He was fighting the world's strongest team, his blokes were being bottled and barracked and bashed. And he was fighting the whole cricket world to establish something he thought would be worthwhile'.

The day after the Guyana riot the Australians returned to the Bourda Ground to hopefully continue the game, the whole place miraculously cleaned up. Chappell was on his way to the press commentary box when he saw Vic Insanally, a local West Indian WSC employee. A rush of blood to the head, Chappell confronted Insanally, accusing him of causing yesterday's mayhem by making the premature announcement about the time for start of play. When Insanally retorted, Chappell punched him in the stomach. A short time later, on his way back to the dressing room, he saw Insanally in a tight huddle with a few officials. Back in the Australian dressing room Chappell told Richie Robinson, 'I think we've got a problem. And I think I'm the cause of the problem'.

Sure enough he was charged with assault and abusive language. The story swept the cricket world, along with banner headlines, and a few days later he was forced to write an apology (penned by his solicitor) and appear before a magistrate. Chappell, determined, stubborn, was on his way to practice when he detoured to go to court, arriving in shorts and a sloppy top. His solicitors were aghast – you can't appear looking like that! It'll look like contempt of court and we'll never get you out of here! Chappell swapped trousers with Austin Robertson. He was fined US$25 on each charge, and the tour continued.

Kerry must have taken note of the wings falling off his players, the injuries, the exhaustion, the stressed behaviour – and the money still pouring out the door. And he saw the ACB and the ICC were hurting, losing money. The future clearly meant both sides continued to get half a limited pie. Kerry knew he couldn't go on killing his guys – some certainty was needed in everyone's lives. That's enough. He stepped back, called in his lawyers and told them to start making deals.

By April 1979 lawyers from both sides were swapping 'in principle' contracts. A short time later Talbot Duckmanton's nightmare came true when the ACB officially withdrew cricket from the ABC and granted it to Channel 9 – the core issue – and the following month the whole deal fell into place. The ACB, full of bravado and righteous indignation, had two years before declared it would never negotiate 'with a gun to its head'. Now, as they ticked paragraphs and okayed points, Kerry smiled at what he had achieved and withdrew his pistol from their temple. He gave his players back to the authorities.

It was agreed that the WSC players, back in the Establishment fold, were not to be victimised, and the coloured clothing for day–night matches – devised for the WSC white ball and because it gave extra spark to the cricket on TV – was to remain part of cricket's new look. At its core, the agreement between Kerry's companies and the ACB had two critical points – Kerry's new corporate body 'PBL Sports' (hived off from his Publishing and Broadcasting Limited), was granted complete and exclusive promotional rights to cricket within Australia, plus television rights, marketing and sponsorship for the next ten years. The company also got a share in gate receipts and a slice of the television action on all matches played inside and outside Australia by the Australian XI. After that the financial deal became complex and labyrinthine, with the ACB given the onerous task of organising cricket tours each season and Kerry the task of doing well out of them. Money flowed both ways, depending on tour profits. If a tour went badly Kerry had to kick in, but this was capped. If a tour was a smashing success the ACB paid Kerry, who got blue sky. He had cleaned up, doing much better than he ever could have hoped for in June 1976.

On 30 May 1979 – a day described by Gideon Haigh as 'the cricket equivalent of Munich, 30 September 1938, with Parish as Neville Chamberlain' – Bob Parish, all bold front, faced a mass of journalists, photographers and TV cameramen in the VCA boardroom and stated, 'I am pleased to announce that the agreement between the ACB and PBL Sports Pty Ltd has been signed and will be lodged with the Trade Practices Commissioner'.

It was all over.

★

Kerry went home – to fully pay out his players' contracts and to spend a little time remembering with a warm glow that day back in 1976, in that very same room where Parish had just spoken, when Parish and Steele had disdainfully told him to go away. He had asked them to name their price. The eventual cost to them was far beyond anything either of them could have imagined. No longer was the Establishment the 'sole promoter' of cricket. Its bete noir, the demon 'private promoter', now had immense and profitable sway in the game.

Unlike Kerry, Parish and Steele didn't go straight home – they had work to do. They had to sell the deal to their international constituency. Parish flew off to London to confront a cynical ICC while faxes and phone calls were made to local cricket authorities in India, Pakistan and the West Indies. None of them were particularly happy.

At this moment Bob Parish was on a hiding to nothing. There is no way, given the position WSC had finessed for itself and the unrelenting and unpredictable style of their maverick opponent, that Parish and Ray Steele could have negotiated anything better. They had fought the good fight, but even with the immense citadel of cricket as their redoubt, even armed with the resources and the moral weight of all the official international sporting authorities, they found themselves outplayed. In London the ICC executives, stiff to the last, accepted – as they undoubtedly had to – Parish's deal with WSC. Yet ICC spokesman Jack Bailey couldn't help firing an ungentlemanly rear-guard shot. 'It was hard to avoid the sense of being hijacked twice in a couple of years, first by Packer, now by the ACB,' he said.

The World Series Cricket revolution now simmered down gently, settled, and the following season of 1979–1980 was the 'season of reconciliation'. Like some kind of brat, Kerry had created so much of a stir that those in charge had finally given him what he wanted – and much more.

And cricket, after a few years of hangover from the trauma, forged on into the twenty-first century with Australia as the global powerhouse. Kim Hughes, who did not play WSC, got something of a poisoned chalice, he captained the Australian side as it settled. Hughes played 28 games as captain and won only four, ending his international career in tears. After that 'Captain Grumpy', Alan Border, took the reins and Australia's post-WSC glory days began. The 'ugly Australian' tag continued to be applied to the killers Australia put onto the field under Border, then Mark Taylor, Steve Waugh and Ricky Ponting. The lessons learned in the hot Australian summers of WSC, lessons learned from living and breathing cricket intimately alongside the hard men of the West Indies and World sides, paid off. The Aussie youngsters who had worshipped Ian Chappell, Lillee, Marsh, Lloyd, Richards, Greig, Roberts, stepped up and, like their heroes, took no prisoners, showed no mercy, and enjoyed grinding their enemies into the 22 yards of hard turf. WSC unleashed an extended era of dominance by the Australian XI that even now continues to polarise cricket commentators who are either for or against the win-at-all-cost mentality.

The chaos of the WSC years prompts the question – could something like this happen at any other time in history? Could it happen now?

Of course. There are always those who deal their own cards in business, who ignore convention, history, protocol, and who see the status quo as just another annoying obstacle in their pursuit of what they want. World Series Cricket was, however, a particularly 1970s phenomenon. In 1976 the great game was at a crossroads, primed by its highly conventional past and ready for an unfettered future. The 1970s was the last decade of free-range, seat-of-the-pants, do-it-yourself optimism before technology, globalisation and the culture of blame and complaint altered the landscape forever. It was a messier, altogether more freewheelin' cultural period. When, at this point in history, they stumbled into each other and decided to kick over the traces, Kerry and his cricketers were operating in a world demonstrably more unguarded than the complex business arenas of the 21st century. 'Those were great times,' says one Kerry executive. 'Everybody was earning plenty of money, we were playing hard and we were working hard, everything was going well. You know you'd think we were the young masters of the universe.' The WSC operatives worked for the seventies and the seventies worked for them.

A major result of the cricket war was that money flowed into the game. Here in the twenty-first century we watch international cricket stars on TV and we see in the press how they've just spent three million bucks on a new house. Match fees and sponsorships, appearance fees and canny investments mean the cream of modern cricketers are dealing daily in soccer star or golf pro money. Bingo – the reason they got into WSC in the first place.

WSC expanded the game's demographics to an amazing degree – cricket during the WSC years and for many years following was not only cool but hot. Cricket was different. Lovers of the sport, their numbers swelled by the women now drawn to it, found a new narrative in the game and a new affection for its heroes. In the twenty-first century cricket continued to re-invent itself with the introduction of T20 which truncates cricket into an exciting two and a half hour baseball-like slug-fest, tailor-made for television. Invented in England, it has been embraced with fervour on the sub-continent. Purists turn away in disgust, just as they did all those years ago with the introduction of the one-day game, but as with the one-dayers, the punters lap it up.

Commentators, particularly those who opposed the WSC revolution, have noted that all these changes would have happened anyway. They go further – cricket was already undergoing change, moving towards the future, when Kerry came along. Yes it was, but glacially. WSC could have happened at any time, but it wouldn't have happened in quite such an intriguingly gung-ho and spectacular fashion. With WSC cricket broke with the past and, cashed up and happy, roared towards the new century with a spring in its step and a fresh attitude. Kerry got what he wanted. So did the cricketers. And so did cricket.

APPENDIX
THE WSC TEAMS

The Australians

Ian Chappell (C), Greg Chappell, Ray Bright, Trevor Chappell, Ian Davis, Ross Edwards, Gary Gilmour, David Hookes, Martin Kent, Bruce Laird, Rob Langer, Dennis Lillee, Ashley Mallett, Mick Malone, Rodney Marsh, Rick McCosker, Graham McKenzie, Kerry O'Keefe, Len Pascoe, Wayne Prior, Ian Redpath, Richie Robinson, Jeff Thomson, Max Walker, Doug Walters, Graeme Watson, Denis Yagmich.

The West Indians

Clive Lloyd (C), Jim Allen, Richard Austin, Colin Croft, Wayne Daniel, Roy Fredericks, Joel Garner, Lance Gibbs, Gordon Greenidge, Desmond Haynes, Michael Holding, David Holford, Rohan Kanhai, Clive Lloyd, Deryck Murray, Bernard Julien, Collis King, Albert Padmore, Vivian Richards, Andy Roberts, Lawrence Rowe.

The World

Tony Greig (C) (England), Zaheer Abbas (Pakistan), Dennis Amiss (England), Taslim Arif (Pakistan), Eddie Barlow (South Africa), Denys Hobson (South Africa), Asif Iqbal (Pakistan), Garth Le Roux (South Africa), Imran Khan (Pakistan), Majid Khan (Pakistan), Alan Knott (England), Javed Miandad (Pakistan), Mushtaq Mohammad (Pakistan), Safraz Nawaz (Pakistan), Graeme Pollock (South Africa), Mike Procter (South Africa), Haroon Rashid (Pakistan), Clive Rice (South Africa), Barry Richards (South Africa), John Snow (England), Derek Underwood (England), Kepler Wessels (South Africa), Bob Woolmer (England).

ACKNOWLEDGMENTS

The publisher kindly acknowledges the following for their permission to reproduce extracts:

Eric Beecher for permission to quote from *The Cricket Revolution* by Eric Beecher (Newspress, 1978)

Henry Blofeld for permission to quote from *The Packer Affair* by Henry Blofeld (Collins, London, 1978)

Melbourne University Press for permission to quote from *The Cricket War: The Inside Story of Kerry Packer's World Series Cricket* by Gideon Haigh (Melbourne University Press, 1993)

Warner Chappell Music Australia Pty Ltd (APRA) for permission to reproduce lyrics from *C'mon Aussie, C'mon* by Allan Johnston & Alan Morris.

BIBLIOGRAPHY

Barry, Paul 1993, *The Rise and Rise of Kerry Packer*, Bantam, Sydney.

Beecher, Eric 1978, *The Cricket Revolution*, Newspress, Melbourne.

Benaud, Richie 1998, *Anything but ... An Autobiography*, Hodder & Stoughton, London.

Blofeld, Henry 1978, *The Packer Affair*, Collins, London.

Caro, Andrew 1979, *With a Straight Bat*, The Sales Machine, Hong Kong.

Chappell, Ian 1992, *The Cutting Edge*, Swan Publishing, Nedlands, WA.

Forsyth, Christopher 1978, *The Great Cricket Hijack*, Widescope Publishers, Camberwell, Victoria.

Greig, Tony with Alan Lee 1980, *Tony Greig: My Story*, Stanley Paul, London.

Haigh, Gideon 1993, *The Cricket War: The Inside Story of Kerry Packer's World Series Cricket*, Melbourne University Press, Melbourne.

Lillee, Dennis 1984, *Over and Out*, Methuen, Sydney.

Lister, Simon 2007, *Supercat: The Authorised Biography of Clive Lloyd*, Fairfield Books, Fairfield Park, Bath.

McDonald, Trevor 1985, *Clive Lloyd: The Authorised Biography*, Granada, London.

McFarline, Peter 1977, *A Game Divided*, Hutchison Group, Melbourne.

Martin-Jenkins, Christopher 1977, *The Jubilee Tests: England v Australia 1977 and the Packer Revolution*, Macdonald and Jane's, London.

Richards, Vivian 1991, *Hitting Across the Line: An Autobiography*, Pan Macmillan Australia, Sydney.